STELLWAGEN BANK

(Irene Seipt)

STELLWAGEN BANK

A Guide to the Whales, Sea Birds, and
Marine Life of the Stellwagen Bank
National Marine Sanctuary

NATHALIE WARD

Center for Coastal Studies
Provincetown, Massachusetts

DOWN EAST BOOKS
Camden, Maine

Copyright © 1995 by Center for Coastal Studies,
Provincetown, Massachusetts
Book design by Edith Allard
Color separations by Piguet Graphics
Printed at Everbest Printing, Hong Kong, through
Four Colour Imports, Louisville, Ky.

9   8   7   6   5   4   3   2

Down East Books / Camden, Maine 04843

Center for Coastal Studies
59 Commercial Street
P.O. Box 1036
Provincetown, MA 02657
(508) 487-3622

Library of Congress Cataloging-in-Publication Data
Ward, Nathalie, 1951–
    Stellwagen Bank: a guide to the whales, sea birds, and
marine life of of the Stellwagen Bank National Marine
Sanctuary / Nathalie Ward
        p.   cm.
    ISBN 0-89272-336-X : $14.95
    1. Marine fauna—Stellwagen Bank.   2. Sea birds—
Stellwagen Bank.   3. Stellwagen Bank.   I. Title
    QL128.W37   1994
    591.974—dc20   94-31840
                                        CIP

THIS BOOK IS DEDICATED TO THE Stellwagen Bank Coalition of over one hundred organizations and individuals that worked in cooperation for over ten years to ensure the designation of Stellwagen Bank and its surrounding waters as the first national marine sanctuary in New England.

The publication of this book was made possible through the generous support of the Center for Coastal Studies members; the Jessie B. Cox Charitable Trust; the Davis Conservation Foundation; Ruth Hiebert, Center patron; the Seth Sprague Educational and Charitable Foundation; and Bank of Boston—The Private Bank.

BANK OF BOSTON
THE PRIVATE BANK

CONTENTS

PERSONS INTERESTED IN LEARNING MORE ABOUT THE STELLWAGEN BANK NATIONAL MARINE SANCTUARY MAY CONTACT THE SANCTUARY HEADQUARTERS IN PLYMOUTH, MASSACHUSETTS, AT (508) 747-1691.

PREFACE

I N 1854, AFTER COUNTLESS HOURS AT SEA taking
soundings of Massachusetts Bay and adjacent waters,
Captain Henry Stellwagen wrote in his diary, "I consider I have made an important discovery in the location
of a fifteen fathom bank lying in a line between Cape
Cod and Cape Ann." These few words encapsulate our
intent upon writing this book on Stellwagen Bank
National Marine Sanctuary—to provide a guide of discovery to the astonishing mosaic of marine life and to
the timeless geological and biological features of the
Bank.

Nathalie F.R. Ward,
author and project editor
David L. DeKing,
Executive Director, Center for
Coastal Studies

The guide was designed to depict the alchemy of
change in Stellwagen Bank's ecosystem—How do the
various life forms of the Bank interact with one another?
Why do fish, seabirds, and whales come to the Bank year
after year? What is a day in the life of Stellwagen Bank
National Marine Sanctuary like? Then, the task set before us was how to create a vivid picture of wonders unseen or scarcely imagined—a world seldom witnessed
because the topside view is often a faceless ocean.

We wanted to create a book that described how marine life and people used the Bank—a habitat use guide.
We knew our text would be complemented by illustrations and photographs, and could easily be augmented
by various identification guides. The best way to cover
the wide range of topics that a guide of this type requires
was to invite many individuals, representing various spe-
cialties and relationships to the Stellwagen Bank Sanctuary, to contribute as authors, consultants, and reviewers.
We are extremely grateful to all the collaborators.

We hope that the guide will stimulate your imagination, confirm your curiosity and love of wild places, and
lead you on your own path of discovery.

ACKNOWLEDGMENTS

I AM INDEBTED TO A GREAT MANY PEOPLE. Without their help and encouragement, this book would never have been possible.

My research on Captain Henry H. Stellwagen was accomplished with the assistance of James Cheevers (Senior Curator at Annapolis Naval Academy), who provided me with copies of Captain Henry Stellwagen's diaries; and Marjorie Ciarlante (National Archives, Washington, D.C.), Melanie Jenard, and Steve Morrison, who supplied me with microfilm of Stellwagen's original manuscripts and charts. A special thank you to Captain Stellwagen's descendants—Thomas Stellwagen, Sr., Thomas Stellwagen, Jr., Elizabeth McCurtan, Barbara Karison, and Horace Stellwagen—for their gracious help in making historical documents and photographs available.

I am indebted to Robert N. Oldale for supplying the information for "The Geology of Stellwagen Bank," and taking the time to explain the geological theories of the formation of Stellwagen Bank in painstaking detail; to Richard Signell, Evelyn Right, David Foster and Christopher Polloni (the United States Geologic Survey, Woods Hole, Massachusetts) who provided computer-generated images of the Bank which were adapted for illustrations.

I would like to thank Stuart Frank, Julie Heller, and Phillip Bergen for letting me into the vaults and taking me back a hundred years to find the paintings for "Historic Departure Points."

I am especially grateful to Jon Witman (Northeastern University Marine Science Center) and Peter Auster (NOAA's Underwater Research Center at the University of Connecticut) whose extensive acquaintance with the marine fauna of the Gulf of Maine helped me identify the invertebrate species to be included in the guide. Additionally, Tracy Villereal (University of Massachusetts), Richard Harbison (Woods Hole Oceanographic Institution), Paul Hargraves (University of Rhode Island), and Brad Barr and Anne Smrcina of the Stellwagen Bank National Marine Sanctuary (Plymouth, Massachusetts) provided technical assistance.

I would like to express my heartfelt gratitude to Wayne Petersen (Massachusetts Audubon) for generously giving his time to reading the "Sea Birds" chapter, catching errors, supplying new information, assisting with the choice of photographs and editing captions. Without his expertise and steady encouragement, the seabird chapter would not have spread its wings. I also wish to thank Kyle Jones (Cape Cod National Seashore) and Irene Seipt, who passed on many useful suggestions in the fledgling stages of the chapter's production.

In writing "Fish and Fishermen," I would have been lost without the ongoing review and instructive suggestions of Molly Benjamin and Frank Mirarchi. Both were invaluable as consultants to ensure that the chapter speak for fishermen—in content and flavor. To Molly: I salute you for keeping me afloat, for your dogged edits and jolly humor throughout the project. To Frank: I would like to express appreciation for your sincere and constant effort to help produce a stellar product. I would also like to thank the following individuals for their contributions: Peter Auster, Marvin Grosslein of the Northeast Division of the National Marine Fisheries Service (NMFS), and Anne Richards (NMFS) for reviewing the chapter for technical accuracy and making helpful comments; Don Flesher for taxonomic corrections. Thanks are also due for section reviews by Bob MacKinnon and Steve Drew (Manomet Observatory and NMFS Observer Program)—gill netting; Jelle Atema and Christy Karavanich (Marine Biological Laboratory)—lobsters; Frank Almeida, Bob Greenfield, and Gary Burnett (NMFS)—aging fish; Brad Chase (Cat Cove Marine Laboratory), who supplied much of the information for the section on bluefin tuna; Marvin Grosslein and Frank Mirarchi for mini lessons in genetics and discussing ideas for "What Controls the Abundance of Marine Fish?"

I am grateful to the many friends who spent long hours, on many occasions, discussing how "Whales, Porpoises, and Dolphins" could best be presented. Their many years of observing whales combined with their fertile imaginations provided me with fresh insights and new information. I would like to thank Laurie Goldman, Scott Kraus, Marilyn Marx, and Stormy Mayo for their review of the North Atlantic right whale section; Margaret Murphy for adding to my knowledge of minke whales; Irene Seipt for getting me to notice subtleties of fin whale behavior and for sharing with me her delight in the natural world; Kurt Fristrup, Peter Tyack, and Bill Watkins for explaining again and again the physics of acoustics and echolocation; Russell DeConti, David Mattila, and Dave Wiley for lively discussions and reviewing selected species accounts; Irene Briga for reminding me that I might have been a four-toed ungulate at one time; and, an extended thanks to Regina Asmutis, Lisa Baraff, Bob Bowman, Colleen Coogan, Mary Ann Dare, Steve Frohock, Andy Read, Butch Rommel, Bill Rossiter, Trevor Spradlin, and Richard Sears for their suggestions and ongoing assistance. For reviewing, editing, and making helpful comments on the entire chapter, I would like to thank Carole Carlson, Phil Clapham, Nancy Flasher, Peter Tyack, Mason Weinrich, and Sharon Young. To all of you, I tip my sunglasses in salute.

I am grateful to Al Avellar's interesting and good-humored conversations which provided the information for "Al Avellar, the Pioneer." Parts of the section were adapted from Seth Rolbein's article "Whalewatching" in the *Boston Herald*. As well, a hearty thanks to Stan Tavares, Ronnie Hunter, and Paul Quintal for providing me with sea legs for so many years.

For the chapters "Seals," "Sea Turtles," and "Conservation" I would like to thank the following reviewers, each of whom gave the manuscript a fresh slant: Irene Seipt, Sharon Young, Phil Clapham, Karen Steuer, Bob Prescott, Michael Payne, and Russell DeConti.

A special thank you goes to Anne Stern for over-the-shoulder edits throughout the project; to Lynn Hiller for proofing the manuscript in its final stages; to Evelyn Gaudiano, who provided endless hours of word processing; to Gail Enos for providing background research on historical harbors; to Charles Westcott for keeping track of all the accounting; to Kathy Shorr for preliminary editing and countless suggestions for sources of information, and to Gibbs Ferris for her graphic wizardry. The list would not be complete without extending my gratitude to Nancy Ludlow, who copy edited the entire manuscript. At Down East Books, thanks go to Tom Fernald, publisher, for taking on this project, to Karin Womer, editor, and to Edith Allard, freelance graphic designer.

I graciously extend a hearty thank you to David De-King, Executive Director of the Center for Coastal Studies, for dropping this project on my lap. His energetic spirit and ongoing encouragement kept my mind flowing and my hands typing throughout the project.

I would also like to thank the photographers and artists whose work on these pages has awakened an admiration for nature's handiwork.

And with good cheer, an everlasting thank you to my mother and father, Ann and Peter Ward, for always encouraging me to seek rewards that might come from taking adventurous risks.

And finally, at home by the campfire, I can answer my daughter Aanjes' perpetual question: "Is it done yet?"

"Yes, it's baked just right."

And I hope that the reader may receive a tithe of the pleasure that the book's preparation has given me.

—Nathalie F. R. Ward

FOREWORD

Sherrard Foster
Project Manager, Stellwagen
Bank Sanctuary, Sanctuaries
and Reserves Division, NOAA
Charles "Stormy" Mayo
Senior Scientist, Center for
Coastal Studies

ONE AUGUST NIGHT IN 1982, we sat in the upstairs offices at the Center for Coastal Studies in Provincetown, on Cape Cod, to put finishing touches on a proposal to designate Stellwagen Bank as a National Marine Sanctuary. The National Oceanic and Atmospheric Administration (NOAA) had invited the public to nominate marine areas for consideration as new sanctuaries to be added to the existing system of ocean sites.

We knew that Stellwagen Bank, rich in living resources, deserved the national recognition that sanctuary status would provide. Much to our delight, the nomination was accepted. In 1983, Stellwagen Bank was added to NOAA's list of marine sites which met the basic criteria for consideration as potential national marine sanctuaries.

We were thrilled when active candidacy finally came in 1989, a result of a congressional mandate that a study on the Stellwagen Bank nomination be prepared and submitted to Congress. To those who know about Stellwagen Bank, it came as no surprise that the Bank was designated a National Marine Sanctuary in 1992.

Those familiar with Stellwagen Bank know the importance of the area for feeding activities to a wide variety of large and small marine mammals, such as whales, dolphins, porpoises, and seals. But in addition, one may also see pelagic birds and sea turtles associated with the area. Beneath the surface, a diversity of groundfish, pelagic fishes, and invertebrates has provided livelihood for fishermen since the time of the Colonists.

Today, the Bank is still a delicate habitat of great richness. To see Stellwagen Bank now recognized for its value to the nation is gratifying for all who worked so many years to protect this special resource.

John Kerry
Gerry E. Studds
Washington, D.C., 1993

A S MEMBERS OF CONGRESS, we are aware that not all issues are broadly and enthusiastically supported by a majority of our constituents. In the Senate and the House of Representatives, we weigh our decisions carefully, knowing that across one state or throughout a single Congressional district it is highly unlikely that all of the people we represent will see eye-to-eye on any given subject. In Massachusetts, however, we have had the pleasure of being able to champion an issue that has had almost universal support: the designation of the Stellwagen Bank National Marine Sanctuary.

The vitality of Stellwagen Bank has been increasingly threatened by a variety of human activities. In 1988, when the construction of an artificial island supporting a hotel and casino complex was proposed for the Bank, letters poured into our offices from fishermen and whalewatchers, from scientists and environmentalists, boaters and schoolchildren. Their response was unanimous: Stellwagen Bank is a very, very special part of the world's oceans—*protect it.* The resulting congressional action brought Stellwagen to the top of the marine sanctuary designation list.

During the designation process, other threats became more apparent, including pollution in Massachusetts Bay, at-sea disposal of dredged materials, and the potential for offshore mineral and gravel mining. Again, the citizens we represent made their positions clear: Stellwagen Bank is a home for commercially valuable fisheries and a feeding ground for endangered whales—*protect them.* Congressional action resulted in a designation with tough provisions designed to save the fragile environment of the Bank, and to ensure long-term protection and management of its resources.

Those of us who have visited Stellwagen Bank to fish for tuna, watch whales, or relish the sunset have enjoyed the rare privilege of glimpsing a world that humans still do not fully understand. Most of the intricate connections between the sea and its inhabitants remain a mystery to us. As a result, we have frequently abused this precious marine environment by using it as a dumping ground for toxic and human waste, poisoning its inhabitants with chemicals, overfishing its once-abundant resources, and now, threatening its delicately balanced ecosystem with global climate change.

Fortunately, it is not too late to save our oceans for the enjoyment of future generations. In the United States, the National Marine Sanctuary Program serves as a model on which other nations can build to conserve their own marine resources. The program is an integral part of our nation's efforts to promote, protect, and enhance the invaluable marine environments that are part of our common natural heritage. The national marine sanctuary system, like our system of national parks, includes a startling diversity of habitats and animals. Marine sanctuaries are windows to the sea—valuable educational tools that bring humans face to face with sea turtles, dolphins, and other marine wildlife in their natural habitat. No substitute exists for this kind of education.

The Stellwagen Bank National Marine Sanctuary adds a real gem to the sanctuary program. We are proud to have played a role in its protection.

SENATOR JOHN KERRY, of Massachusetts, through the Marine Sanctuaries Reauthorization Act of 1988, directed the Secretary of Commerce to move Stellwagen Bank from the Site Evaluation List to Active Candidate status. Senator Kerry was also instrumental in the passage of the National Marine Sanctuaries Reauthorization and Improvement Act of 1992, which designated Stellwagen Bank as a National Marine Sanctuary.

CONGRESSMAN GERRY E. STUDDS, of Massachusetts, is an ardent supporter in Congress of a strong marine sanctuary program and is an author of the National Marine Sanctuaries Reauthorization and Improvement Act of 1992, the law which designates the Stellwagen Bank National Marine Sanctuary.

*Naked sea butterflies (*Clione limacina*) measure about one and a half inches (3.7 cm) long. These shell-less gastropods, called pteropods, make up part of the plankton population. Two extensions of its foot (the "wings") are used for swimming. Side by side with their winglike flaps wrapped around one another, two sea butterflies mate.* (Wes Pratt)

*Beroe's comb jelly (*Beroe cucmis*) has a flattened saclike body with a broad mouth. Unlike jellyfish, which move with their mouths underneath or behind, comb jellies advance mouth-end forward. Mature individuals reach a size of about eight inches (20 cm).* (Richard Harbison)

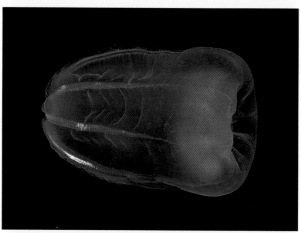

*The long, trailing tentacles of the sea gooseberry (*Pleurobrachia pileus*) capture fish eggs and larvae, and other planktonic organisms. This comb jelly measures about an inch (25 mm) in diameter.* (Larry Madin)

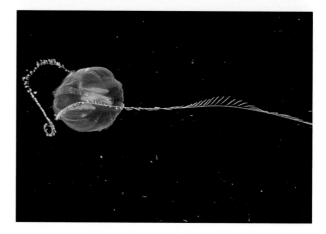

The Pageant of Life

BEGINNING IN THE FIRST SUNLIT FATHOM and reaching down into the darkness, Stellwagen Bank National Marine Sanctuary is home to a vast citizenry.

Life flourishes. Virtually every rock and crevice has its crawling, creeping, or sedentary tenants. Sluggish creatures exist on the pallid sands and mud bottom in a slow-motion world where journeys are made in inches. A tubeworm feeds and breathes with fountainlike appendages waving in the current. Disturbed by a sudden movement, a whelk retracts into its shell and battens down the hatch. Beneath the surface of sand and silt are numerous mansions—holes of moon snails, burrows of crabs, mazes of sea worms, and hideaways of surf clams. Shipwrecks and their ghosts are found here, too.

Unlike bottom dwellers fettered to the sea floor, free-swimming animals explore new horizons. Sand lance swim over the sea floor in compact formation, like well-disciplined armies. Twenty feet (6 meters) above, pilot whales chase schools of transparent squid. Floating communities of microscopic plants drift in the restless currents. Along with these ride an infinite number of intermediate forms: the larvae of lobsters, sea urchins, and many kinds of young fish.

A gust of wind shimmies across the water's surface. Sky and sea mingle hazily, showing the first flush of dawn on the gray crumpled water. In the distance, a dragger steams for port; it has been fishing the Bank through the night. Herring gulls follow in its wake, calling out with variant sounds until all blend into one great monotone.

This is the home of many living things, an animate panorama affected by the rhythmic rise and fall of the tides, the moving sea.

*On its rubberlike gray foot, a northern moon snail (*Lunatia heros*) creeps along a sandy bottom studded with sand dollars. The muscular foot allows the moon snail to plow underneath the sand in search of other mollusks, such as clams, upon which it feeds. It drills a hole through the shell of its victim with its toothed tongue, or radula, and then sucks out the contents. Size: five inches (12.7 cm)* (Jon Witman)

*Sticking its head out of a leathery tube, a plumed worm (*Diopatria cuprea*) tentatively explores the world beyond with its five long sensory antennae.* (Wes Pratt)

An Inheritance

"The created world is but a small parenthesis in eternity."

—Sir Thomas Browne

The Stellwagen Bank National Marine Sanctuary encompasses 638 square nautical miles (2189 sq. km.). On a vaster scale, it is part of the Gulf of Maine ecosystem. Formed by the relentless alchemy of glaciers, wind, and water, Stellwagen Bank had its geological beginnings some twenty thousand years ago during the last great ice age.

The sea spreads out before you, miles and miles of flatness. Below, the sea floor tells a different story. The Bank's broad, sandy bottom is scattered with ridges and troughs, reminders of vanished epochs when the seas rode lower and belonged to the land. Adjacent to the Bank, steep canyons and gorges cut into the ocean floor. The push and pull of tides, currents, and storms reshape the bottom each day.

Within this intricate network of natural processes, tiny animals and plants abound, forming the basis for the endless food web for larger animals. Each living creature is at once hunted and hunter, food and feeder. When an animal dies, its remains fall to the bottom where they are devoured by scavengers or decomposed by bacteria. Upwelling currents then bring the decomposed matter, also known as detritus, to the surface

Stellwagen Bank is a submerged plateau in the Gulf of Maine, located approximately 26 miles (42 km) east of Boston, 6 miles (10 km) north of Race Point (Provincetown), Massachusetts, and 7 miles (11 km) southeast of Gloucester, Massachusetts. The glacially deposited bank forms a narrow triangle, roughly 18.5 miles (30 km) in length and 6.25 miles (10 km) in width at the southern end, narrowing to 2.5 miles (4 km) to the north.

Depths for the Bank's shallowest areas are 71.5 feet (22 meters), with areas of the upper plateau recording depths close to 108 feet (33 meters). The sides drop off steeply on the western edge, in Stellwagen Basin, to over 328 feet (100 meters). On the seaward side, the drop is more gradual.

The Sanctuary encompasses approximately 638 square nautical miles (2189 sq km). (E. Paul Oberlander)

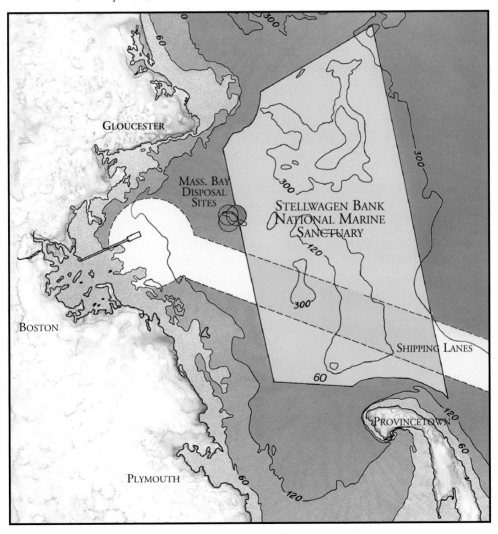

where it provides fertilizer for the plants. Thus the food web is renewed.

For centuries, our ingenuity has allowed us to harvest fish and shellfish living in the Bank's nutrient-rich waters. Today, fishing fleets from numerous Massachusetts ports continue to fish for many commercially important groundfish such as Atlantic cod, silver hake, yellowtail flounder, and ocean pout, and economically important shellfish species, including American lobster, sea scallops, squid, and ocean quahogs. In addition, private boaters seek out giant bluefin tuna and striped bass. Charter fishing boats and whalewatching boats provide easy access for exploring Sanctuary waters. The Bank is a busy place.

Myriads of sea birds can be found on the Bank throughout the year. Migratory species visit the area during their travels, including gannets, shearwaters, storm petrels, fulmars, phalaropes, and alcids, such as puffins and razorbills.

The shallow waters of Stellwagen Bank attract a variety of whales, porpoises, and dolphins. Three endangered species—the humpback whale, the North Atlantic right whale, and the finback whale—are sighted there. Many nonendangered species, such as minke and pilot whales, harbor porpoise, and Atlantic white-sided dolphins, also visit the Bank. Other marine animals that have been sighted include harbor and gray seals, and endangered sea turtles.

The complexity and wonder of the Sanctuary reside not only in what we can see, but also in what we cannot—the subtle streaming of its currents, the pulsing of its tides, and the invisible hosts of marine life that call the Bank home.

Time ticks away, shaping the present and future of Stellwagen Bank. We often view the sea we have inherited as a malleable and transient commodity belonging to us. We use it, often abuse it, and then move on, unaware of the legacy we leave behind. When we see the ocean as a community to which we all belong, we may begin to see it with love and respect—a treasured inheritance.

"Waste not, want not." A sea raven (Hemitripterus americanus) *swallows a not so fortunate lobster in one gulp.* (Peter Auster)

THE GEOLOGY OF STELLWAGEN BANK

A MILLION AND A HALF YEARS AGO, Stellwagen Bank and the entire Gulf of Maine were a dry coastal plain marked by gentle hills, lowland swamps, and marshes. Then the glaciers arrived, a series of massive ice sheets that rolled over the North American continent, carving out the geology of Stellwagen Bank as we know it today.

If one looks at the Stellwagen Bank region of the Gulf of Maine, the Bank appears to be a northward extension of outer Cape Cod and its adjacent sea floor. This is more than a coincidence, since the Bank and outer Cape Cod share much of the same geologic history.

Like Cape Cod, Stellwagen Bank owes its present shape to the last continental glacier and to associated changes in sea level. The basic difference is that Stellwagen Bank was submerged by the rise in sea level following the retreat of the last continental ice sheet, while Cape Cod remained above sea level. The submergence of the Bank has hidden much of the evidence of its origin, but studies of the geology of the outer Cape provide the necessary clues about how and when Stellwagen Bank was formed.

Information supplied by Robert Oldale, United States Geological Survey

The Laurentide Ice Sheet

The most important agent in the formation of Stellwagen Bank was the Laurentide ice sheet, the last continental glacier in North America. The Laurentide, named after the St. Lawrence region of Canada from which it came, formed about seventy-five thousand years ago when energy from the sun reaching the earth was less than it is today.

Glaciers and ice sheets form when the climate is cold

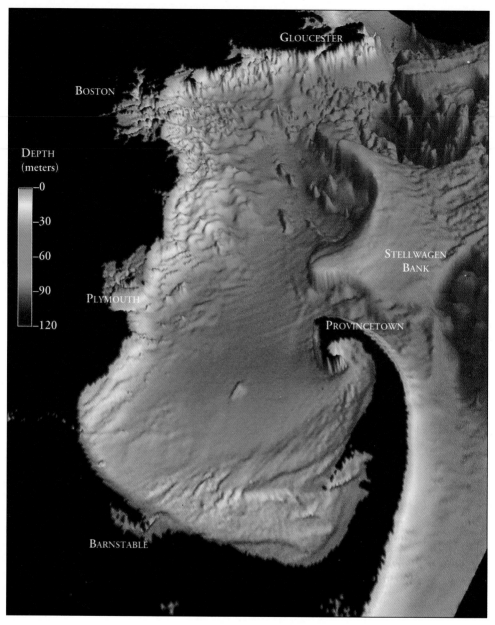

DEPTH
(meters)

—0

—30

—60

—90

—120

GLOUCESTER

BOSTON

PLYMOUTH

STELLWAGEN
BANK

PROVINCETOWN

BARNSTABLE

(Map courtesy of Richard Signell, U.S. Geological Survey)

enough that each year more snow falls during the cold months than can be melted during the warmer months. As the snow accumulates year by year, the lower part is compressed into ice. Over hundreds or thousands of years, the mass of ice and snow becomes thick enough to flow—or move in the form of a glacier or ice sheet.

The Laurentide Ice Sheet advanced out of Canada about twenty-five thousand years ago and reached southern New England about twenty-one thousand years ago, scraping and chiseling the land as it advanced. Shortly after its arrival there, the ice sheet began its retreat, as melting at the glacier's edge exceeded the advance of the ice. By about eighteen thousand years ago, the ice sheet had retreated to the vicinity of Cape Cod.

During the retreat, or deglaciation, the edge of the ice sheet was scalloped into several glacial lobes, or bulges. There were two prominent lobes. The Cape Cod Bay lobe lay to the west of outer Cape Cod, occupying Cape Cod Bay. The South Channel lobe extended on the east of the lower Cape, covering an area now bordered by Martha's Vineyard, Nantucket, and the large submerged area called Georges Bank.

The retreat of the lobes was not synchronous. It is believed that the Cape Cod Bay lobe, occupying Stellwagen Basin, retreated first. There is direct evidence from geologic samples of foraminifera—microscopic, hard-shelled, single-celled animals found in the glacial mud deposits—that the ice-free part of Stellwagen Basin was replaced by an arm of the sea. Radiocarbon dating of these animals indicates that the sea had entered the basin by eighteen thousand years ago, and that Stellwagen Bank was formed about that time.

With progressive thawing, meltwater streams flowed westward from the South Channel lobe, depositing glacial sediments, such as sand and gravel, in the sea and on the Bank top. The glacial formation of Stellwagen Bank ceased once the South Channel lobe retreated into the Gulf of Maine. Removal of the mile-high ice load allowed the depressed earth's crust to rebound, and shortly after the continental glacier waned, sea level fell some distance below the Bank. The glacial sand and

Facing page: *Stellwagen Bank is the most prominent submarine feature in Massachusetts Bay. Located just north of outer Cape Cod, the broad, shallow plateau of the Bank (yellow) slopes gently eastward. To the west, the Bank is bordered by the deeper water of Stellwagen Basin.*

This computer generated map shows the depth (in meters) of the ocean floor on and around Stellwagen Bank. The deepest water is shown in blue; the shallowest, along the coast, is in red. This perspective view of Massachusetts Bay is vertically exaggerated 100 times.

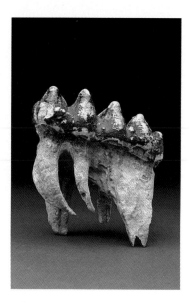

The recovery of this mastodon tooth from Stellwagen Basin by a local draggerman supports the belief that at one time Stellwagen Bank was dry land and may have been the home for Amerindian populations. (Tom Kleindinst)

gravel that make up Stellwagen indicate that, during its formation, the Bank top was most likely above sea level.

Sea Level Rise and Fall

The sea is the other important agent in the construction of Stellwagen Bank. As the Laurentide ice sheet grew, water was removed from the ocean basins and sea level fell. Beyond the glacier, shorelines regressed and coastal plains emerged from the sea. At maximum glaciation— about twenty-one thousand years ago—sea level fell about 295 feet (90 meters) below its present point.

Twelve thousand years ago, the Bank remained above the sea and probably looked much like the glacial outwash plains of outer Cape Cod today, complete with kettle holes, marine scarps, and coastal marshes. The Bank may even have had a dry-land connection to lower Cape Cod, or it may have been separated from the Cape by a broad shallow strait in Little Stellwagen Basin.

As the continental glacier melted and withdrew, water returned to the ocean basins and the seas rose to cover the land. Continued rise in sea level eventually drowned the Bank, perhaps about ten thousand years ago, covering the Bank to its present depth. Sea level is still rising today, but much more slowly than in the past. Presently, the water depth over Stellwagen Basin increases about four inches (10 cm) every hundred years.

Over time, most of the finer-grained materials have been carried away by currents and deposited in basin areas on either side of the Bank, leaving predominantly coarse-grained sand with some occasional rocky outcrops.

Stellwagen Bank, approximately eighteen thousand years old, is an offshoot of the two-hundred-million-year-old Atlantic Ocean. Like Cape Cod, it is a comparatively young and transitory geographic feature of the North American landscape.

STELLWAGEN
BANK

SEA FLOOR

GLACIAL DEPOSITS

COASTAL PLAIN STRATA

FOUNDATION / BEDROCK

A hypothetical geologic cross-section (facing north), based on seismic soundings, shows the structure of Stellwagen Bank. (Jennifer Potthoff)

The Foundation. *The rock beneath Stellwagen Bank is probably 150 million to 500 million years old. The oldest rocks formed when there was little life on the planet; other rocks formed when life first became abundant in the sea and later, during the age of dinosaurs. This basement rock, or bedrock, is 400 to 600 feet (120 to 180 meters) below the surface of the Bank.*

These rocks contain a record of global tectonics—the movement of huge plates of the earth's crust. Over vast amounts of time, continents broke apart and moved away from each other to form ocean basins, then collided together again to form mountain ranges. It is likely that some of the basement rocks beneath Stellwagen Bank date from the time when the Atlantic Ocean first formed, over two hundred million years ago.

Coastal Plain Strata—*deposits between 250 and 400 feet (76 and 122 meters) thick composed mostly of loose gravel, sand, silt, and clay—are thought to occur beneath Stellwagen Bank. These deposits were formed between 5 million and 140 million years ago. About 5 million years ago, sea level fell, and Stellwagen Bank began to take shape as the streams and rivers eroded away the coastal plain deposits adjacent to the Bank.*

Glacial Deposits. *During the 1.5 million years of the most recent ice age, the Gulf of Maine and the Stellwagen region were undoubtedly glaciated many times. Sand and gravel make up the bulk of the glacial deposits. These deposits, up to 400 feet (122 meters) thick, mostly overlie coastal plain deposits, though in a few places they lie directly on the basement rock.*

Sea Floor. *The sea floor of Stellwagen Bank is made up primarily of sand and gravel. Coarser sand and gravel flank the eastern edge of the Bank. A silt and clay bottom is common in Stellwagen Basin, on the western edge of the Bank.*

Henry S. Stellwagen (1809–66) discovered Stellwagen Bank in October 1854, while conducting a survey of Massachusetts Bay. (Seth Rolbein)

A NAMESAKE: CAPTAIN HENRY S. STELLWAGEN

In 1853, Henry S. Stellwagen, an accomplished hydrographer for the U.S. Navy and an assistant in the Coast Survey, received orders from Superintendent Alexander Dallas Bache to conduct soundings in Massachusetts Bay. On October 22, 1854, Stellwagen wrote to the superintendent:

> . . . I consider I have made an important discovery in the location of a 15 fathom bank lying in a line between Cape Cod and Cape Ann—with 40 and 50 fathoms inside and to the northward of it and 35 fathoms just outside of it. . . . We have traced nearly 5 miles in width and over 6 miles in length, it no doubt extending much further. . . . We are all very much interested in pursuing the discovery still further to determine if it is a continuous bank or [a] detached knoll. It is not on any chart I have been able to procure, Blunts shows deep water in every direction.

As his investigations continued, he wrote (October 27):

> I find the Bank is known by [the] vague term of Middle Bank but little is ascertained about it except that it is a good fishing ground.

Stellwagen made detailed accounts and astoundingly accurate observations in his journals as he sampled bottom sediments with a sounding apparatus he invented, known as the Stellwagen Cap.

> The soundings on [the] northern end of bank indicate rocky bottom though the Stellwagen sounding cap brought up small pieces of stone and fine black sand . . . the middle and southern parts seem to be generally coarse white sand. . . . the bottom inside in the deep water is generally a green unctuous mud or ooze. The bank front rises gradually from the east but rises very abrupt and steep on its western edge.

Throughout the fall, Stellwagen and his crew continued the survey under adverse weather conditions.

> We have had a continuous succession of gales and fogs and have had to work with the sea and spray flying over the ship and men, and the water freezing on the decks part of the time. . .

Upon completion of the survey, a jubilant Stellwagen wrote again to Bache.

> *Boston Bay Nov 9th 1854*
>
> *My dear Sir:*
>
> *I have to announce to you the completion of the
> examination of a Bank lying just outside of Massa-
> chusetts Bay and in the direct line just outside of
> Boston from the east and southeast directions. . . . We
> have cropped it 6 times and ascertained its width,
> outlines and position with great accuracy and run
> through its whole length twice . . .*
>
> *I consider the promulgation of the discovery a very
> essential thing to navigators and that the knowledge
> of it will highly benefit Commanders and the great
> commercial interest of the City of Boston—and that
> it will serve as an invaluable aid to mariners bound
> in during thick weather by day or night."*
>
> *Should you see proper to secure the Bank as you
> hinted in your letter after me, I shall have no objec-
> tions to fathering it—*
>
> *HSS*

HARBORS

Madeleine Walsh, Urban Harbors Institute, University of Massachusetts, Boston

WHILE OCEANS SEPARATE NATIONS, harbors bring them together. As you begin your voyage to Stellwagen Bank, you will leave from one of New England's many harbors. These sheltered bodies of water, deep enough for ships to moor or anchor in, tell their own history.

The activities of ports and harbors intersect on Stellwagen Bank. Fishermen leave their home ports in search of abundant catches. Tourists venture from local harbors to observe some of the largest creatures on earth—finback and humpback whales. Industrialists ship cargo from Asia, Egypt, and Iceland to the port of Boston. All of these groups, while having different goals, are on the same journey. They pass over Stellwagen Bank and return to their home ports better off for having made the voyage.

Historical Departure Points to Stellwagen Bank

Provincetown Harbor

Clive E. Driver, Historian

Formed by the hook at the tip-end of Cape Cod, Provincetown Harbor was the first landing place of the Mayflower Pilgrims on November 11, 1620. It was described by their leader, William Bradford, as "circled round, except in the entrance, which is about four miles over from land to land; compassed about to the very sea with oaks, pines, juniper, sassafras, and other sweet woods. It is a harbor wherein a thousand sail of ships may safely ride."

Although incorporated in 1727, the town of Provincetown—three miles (4.8 km) long and two

Built in 1851 and owned by Captain John A. Cook until 1919, the sailing bark Greyhound *was one of the last Provincetown whaling ships. This photograph dates from around 1900.* (From the collection of Reginald Cabral)

streets wide—was little more than a seasonal fishing village until after the American Revolution. Even so, by the beginning of the eighteenth century, the forests had all been cut down for housing, fuel, and shipbuilding, and the migrating dunes had begun to drift into the harbor.

During the nineteenth century, Provincetown became a major port. Whaling, which began as an offshore operation, eventually reached all corners of the Atlantic and Pacific oceans. Second only to New Bedford, Provincetown was called home port by 175 whaling ships. An equal number of Grand Banks fishing schooners—some weighing up to 200 tons—left Provincetown in the spring, each carrying 60 to 150 barrels of dry salt from Provincetown's 78 salt works (a series of vats that drew water out of the harbor and, by evaporation, produced salt). As the fish were caught, they were salted down; at the end of the voyage the fish were washed off in the harbor and spread on flakes (racks) to dry. These racks were constructed around nearly every house in town and

A New England Harbor

By looking around a harbor, you can find clues about wind conditions, tidal cycles, and the port's activities. Clues on the water's surface can even tell what is happening underneath. For instance, a large number of brightly colored lobster buoys dotting the surface often indicates a rocky bottom and a healthy lobster population. Hovering and diving sea birds are clues to a momentary supply of schooling fish, such as menhaden, herring, or sand lance.

Wind direction can be discerned by taking note of the ripples or waves on the water's surface or by observing the moored boats; generally, anchored boats head into the wind.

Piers, pilings, boats, bell buoys, and breakwaters all help to define a harbor. Beyond their intended purpose, these features provide a solid foundation in an otherwise constantly shifting environment of water and sand. They also encourage and sustain marine life similar to what you would find on rocky shores.

Notice the pilings—is it high or low tide? Barnacles, blue mussels, sea squirts, and rockweed will most likely be uncovered at low tide. At high tide, visible signs of life are often absent. The shoreline clearly shows the high-water mark by a line of seaweed and sundry ocean giveaways. Keep an eye on the herring gull above you. Watch it shatter a clam by dropping it on the hard surface below to get the food inside the shell.

As you continue your investigation, you can classify the port by the different kinds of boats you see. They probably include fishing, cargo, and recreational vessels. All these components make up the busy life of a harbor.

(Jennifer Potthoff)

every other open space. The shore of the harbor became jammed with all the wharves and buildings needed to support these twin industries—shipbuilding yards, spar shops, ropewalks, blacksmith shops, ship stores, sail lofts, and places where nets were tarred.

Toward the end of the century, however, the market for fresh fish began to exceed that for dried and salt fish. The demand for whale oil declined as kerosene became widely available, and the remaining whalers had to travel farther and farther afield for their catch. Then disaster struck. On November 27, 1898, in the memorable Portland Gale, more than half of Provincetown's fifty-two wharves were destroyed and many boats and lives were lost. A combination of declining markets and lack of major capital prevented the rebuilding of either industry. Fishing now became largely a matter of a trip out at dawn and back at dusk by individual Portuguese fishermen, many of whom had arrived as hands on whaling ships and did not have the funds for larger ventures. Fishing was done with individual handlines or with seine weirs within the harbor.

Provincetown in 1900 had declined to a small, sleepy

A view of Plymouth, Massachusetts, from the beach east of the harbor. Color lithograph after Timothy Barry, 1845. (Collection of Kendall Whaling Museum, Sharon, Massachusetts)

fishing village with a faltering economy and dozens of vacant buildings along the harbor. Then it was rediscovered by groups of artists and writers. Unused harborfront buildings became artists' studios; one became the first home of the Provincetown Players, the birthplace of the American little theater movement.

Today, a small fishing fleet survives. Nearly everyone else in town is dependent on its only other industry—tourism. Whalewatch boats, fishing party boats, and recreational boats dominate the harbor. Most of the buildings in town have been turned into shops, galleries, restaurants, and guest houses. Still nestled along the harbor, the town now attracts tens of thousands of visitors who come to admire what quiet beauty still remains.

Plymouth

Plymouth Harbor immediately conjures up visions of the Mayflower Pilgrims who first came here on the stormy evening of December 9, 1620. Yet the Pilgrims and their rock were only one chapter in the story of Plymouth's harbor.

James W. Baker,
Plimoth Plantation

Plymouth Harbor is formed by two long, sandy spits of land framing a narrow entrance to Massachusetts Bay. Duxbury Beach extends southward to Guernet Point and its lighthouse, then makes a sharp turn west to Saquish Head. Clark's Island rests just inside this hook of land. On the south, Plymouth Beach reaches up from the mouth of the Eel River.

For centuries, the harbor was Plymouth's window on the world. The Pilgrims shipped furs and cod to pay their debts, and cod fishing remained a leading maritime activity into the twentieth century. By the time of the American Revolution, wharves lined the waterfront at the foot of Cole's Hill, and Plymouth's shipping industry grew and flourished during the first half of the nineteenth century. Prolific shipbuilding enterprises in Kingston and Duxbury made Plymouth Harbor famous the world over.

Following the Civil War, however, shipbuilding ceased and shipping declined. Large modern vessels couldn't enter the shallow harbor, despite channels dredged to the town's seven wharves and the Plymouth

Cordage Company. Only the shrinking fishing fleet and the coastal steamers that brought tourists down from Boston remained when, in 1920, the entire waterfront was cleared away for the 1921 Pilgrim Tercentenary.

Since then, Plymouth Harbor has become a departure point for pleasure boating, whalewatching trips, and fishing parties. Summer homes cover Guernet Point and Saquish Head, and Plymouth Beach maintains a sanctuary for endangered terns. There is even a sturdy remnant of Plymouth fishermen still following the age-old call of the fishing banks. The Plymouth of today has not turned her back on the sea.

Boston

Captain Ed Burns,
Boston Harbor Historian

Boston Harbor, an area of about fifty square miles, is bounded by 180 miles of shoreline and dotted with thirty islands. Boston Harbor has always played an important role in New England's history. Before the coming of the first settlers, Native American tribes frequented the harbor islands. Piles of clam shells and other signs provide evidence of their campsites and activities, which included fishing, hunting, and cultivating crops.

The harbor's protected waters provided refuge to the first explorers, and its tributary waters offered transportation routes for the founders of what became Boston and its surrounding villages. These locations, often on hills and peninsulas projecting into the harbor, offered the advantage of easily defensible sites.

During the American Revolution, two thousand of General Washington's troops occupied Dorchester Heights, overlooking the harbor; this defense led to the British evacuation of Boston in March 1776.

Since the city was founded, Boston has flourished as a great port. By 1660, virtually all imports from England to New England passed through Boston Harbor. In the age of sail — 1750 to 1850 — Boston Harbor was the third-busiest harbor in the world. Here were born the clippers, the fastest sailing ships the world would ever see. Boston-built clipper ships plied the trade routes in those days, bringing fish and timber out and returning with gold, silk, tea, and other goods.

Boston Harbor's ghosts could spin exciting yarns. Paul Revere rowed his boat across the harbor to begin his midnight ride. In the War of 1812, Captain James Lawrence lay mortally wounded on the deck of the Chesapeake, just off Boston Light, when he uttered his famous battle cry, "Don't give up the ship."

Since its beginning, Boston Harbor has been a hub of activity. Today, it retains its unique historic character while moving forward.

Gloucester

In 1606, Samuel de Champlain sat on Gloucester's Rocky Neck and drew the first map of Gloucester Harbor. He called it le Beauport, "the beautiful harbor."

Since the first American fishing settlement was established in Gloucester in 1623, fishermen and traders have made it one of the country's busiest and most famous deepwater harbors.

During the first half of the nineteenth century, Gloucester supported both an active fishing industry and

An assortment of carts and drays move merchandise along Broad Street, the waterfront of Boston Harbor, in this 1853 painting by John White Allen. (Courtesy of the Bostonian Society. Photographer R. Cheek.)

Judith McCulloch,
Cape Ann Historical Association

29

a prosperous trade network with the Dutch colony of Surinam. Later in the century, Gloucester turned its attention almost entirely to fishing. It became the center for fisheries under sail, and imposing wooden schooners filled the harbor. Gloucester remains a busy commercial fishing port today.

The schooners also filled the paintings of Gloucester native Fitz Hugh Lane, who has become known all over the world for his luminous maritime scenes. Artists were drawn to Gloucester even before Lane's time because of its natural beauty and the strong images offered by the fishing fleet. Among the artists who came after Lane are Winslow Homer, Maurice and Charles Prendergast, Frank Duveneck, Jane Peterson, John Sloan, and Milton Avery. All these artists have helped to create a compelling visual history of the harbor, which present-day artists continue to develop.

Eastern Point lighthouse at the Dog Bar breakwater marks the end of open ocean and the beginning of the outer harbor. A channel provides access to the inner harbor, the historic center for Gloucester's maritime activity. The city itself commands a hill overlooking the

Looking in toward Gloucester from the outer harbor, Lane provides a sampling of mid-nineteenth–century vessels, including the chebacco boat (center foreground) with its trawl line. Gloucester Harbor, *1852, by Fitz Hugh Lane (1804–65).* (Collection of Cape Ann Historical Association, Gloucester)

harbor, with houses and commercial buildings stretching all the way to the waterfront. Ten Pound Island, with its historic lighthouse, creates a familiar landmark in the harbor.

Over time, the appearance of the harbor has changed. Vincents Cove, a bustling area of wharves and piers early in this century, has been completely filled in. Five Pound Island has disappeared, becoming part of the State Fish Pier project. But Gloucester retains its essential character as a working harbor and offers many reminders of Gloucester's reputation as the continent's most productive nineteenth-century fishing port.

CORMORANTS:
IN PURSUIT OF SUBMARINE CUISINE

In any New England harbor you are certain to see cormorants. Black-bodied, prehistoric looking, cormorants fish for a living. They thrive on the small schooling fish of coastal waters. These long-necked, glossy black birds can be seen perched on rocks, buoys, or pilings between submarine excursions.

Cormorants lack the oil glands that produce the waterproofing oil that protects most aquatic birds from getting drenched. In response to nature's omission, their answer is drip drying—a peculiar habit of sitting with wings outstretched.

These heavy-bodied birds swim half submerged, paddling along with necks extended and bills angled skyward. Without a moment's notice, cormorants can dive below the surface in pursuit of fish. On underwater forays that can last up to half a minute, they swim with their powerful wings and stroke both webbed feet.

They are excellent divers because their bodies are well adapted to swimming underwater and their water permeable feathers reduce their buoyancy. Cormorants have been known to swallow stones to help them gain extra depth. These amazing birds have been found in nets at depths up to 120 feet (37 meters)!

The double-crested cormorant's throat pouch is bright orange. Like other cormorants, it slants its bill upward while swimming. Its long, flexible neck is ideal for darting at prey. (VIREO)

Cormorants have voracious appetites. The name cormorant comes from the Latin *corvus marinus,* translated as "sea raven." Shakespeare called the birds "insatiate," and fishermen once put a bounty on their heads. Their skill at stalking and seizing fish has been exploited in Asia for centuries. Attached to long leashes, and wearing collars that prevent them from swallowing their catch, juvenile cormorants are easily trained to harvest fish for their masters.

Two species of cormorants frequent New England waters. The double-crested cormorant (*Phalacrocorax auritus*), the species most sighted in summer and fall, has a bright orange throat pouch. A discerning eye may notice the source of its name—a small crest or tuft of feathers above each eye that is most prominent during the spring breeding season. The great cormorant (*Phalacrocorax carbo*), primarily a winter

(Sarah Landry)

resident, is the larger of the two local species and may be recognized by its pronounced white throat patch and yellower bill.

Generally, these species are similar in appearance and behavior. Adult birds have a cylindrical bill that is hooked at the tip, a partially naked face with a visible throat pouch, and dark, iridescent black plumage. Their body size may reach lengths up to 3.28 feet (1 meter). Both species are remarkable for their curiously formed feet with all four toes webbed, their long stiff tails, and the absence of exterior nostrils—they breathe through their mouths.

Great cormorants nest in large groups on cliff ledges or rocks, or in bushes on islands in the Gulf of St. Lawrence, while double-crested cormorants breed on many islands in Massachusetts, especially in Boston Harbor. They construct nests from seaweed, sticks, and, often, man-made litter. Parents alternate incubating the eggs for about four weeks. The naked, coal-black hatchlings look like animated rubber toys, but by their tenth week, they're ready to fly.

In the late 1800s, cormorants gained quite a bit of notoriety in New England. Their excrement was highly prized as an organic fertilizer, or guano, and the huge guano deposits found on the coast of South America were harvested by the successful Pacific Guano and Fertilizer Company of Woods Hole, Massachusetts. Today, cormorants still incur the enmity of fishermen, who believe they compete for fish. However, investigations have shown that their effect on fish populations, especially those species sought by humans, is minimal.

Cormorants have a reputation for awkwardness. On takeoff, these birds usually hit the water a few times with their wings before gaining altitude. Often, large numbers of black silhouettes are seen in a low-flying, ragged V-formation, lumbering across the water. We surface dwellers do not always get the best view, however. The agility of cormorants underwater as they wheel and turn with ease in pursuit of their submarine cuisine is a lively contrast to their ungainly stances above the surface.

THE STELLWAGEN BANK ECOSYSTEM

Charles "Stormy" Mayo,
Center for Coastal Studies

STELLWAGEN BANK IS BEST DESCRIBED as a complex system of plants and animals whose lives are interdependent, delicately balanced, and sensitive to a myriad of constantly changing physical and chemical processes. As you look at the sea, this complexity will not be apparent, since the processes of wind and wave and the interaction of the plants and animals are largely hidden. The vitality and richness of the Stellwagen Bank system can be known only if the connections and balances among its many components are understood.

Water Cycles

Water is the essence of the Stellwagen Bank system. Although it is not obvious, the water is constantly moving and changing in ways that fundamentally affect the Bank. Water bathes the Bank, transporting vital plant nutrients and distributing marine animals. Indeed, water is the medium of this system, the primary habitat for some of the most important resources of the region: large fish, plankton, and whales. It is because of the interaction between the physical and biological parts of this environment that the sea is green, that the whales return each year, and that the clams reproduce.

The water of the Stellwagen system has a history, which forms the foundation of what we see today. The water over Stellwagen Bank has flowed down from the colder regions of the Gulf of Maine into Massachusetts Bay, taking weeks to pass along the shores of Maine and New Hampshire to reach the Bank. This Gulf of Maine water starts its journey nutrient-rich, cold, and clean. As it moves along the eastern coastline, it is slowly changed by the infusion of river water, by atmospheric and surface pollutants, and by a variety of human activities. Changes in the chemical and physical characteristics of the water influence, in many ways, the organisms that live on Stellwagen Bank. For example, the amount of oxygen and salt in the water may cause commercially important species of fish to succeed or fail, while the clarity of the surface layer determines how much light is available for marine plants. The levels of oxygen, salt, and light also influence the quality of the bottom habitats of lobsters and crabs.

In addition to the north/south drift of water over the Bank, horizontal currents also influence the area, but to a lesser degree. Fast currents (one to two miles per hour, or 1.6 to 3.2 kph) sweep east and west across the region, driven by the power of the tides. They create areas of turbulence, or "rips," where small fish congregate and sea birds, marine mammals, and large fish feed. At the edges of Stellwagen Bank the shallows block tidal currents and create periodic upwelling and turbulence that is often visible at the surface. During certain times of the year, these upwelling currents bring vital plant nutrients to the surface and trigger the essential seasonal pattern of enrichment of the Bank system.

Hidden from our view are alien worlds. This lobsterlike larva joins the ranks of tiny carnivorous animals that are the lifeblood of oceanic systems. (Larry Madin)

Water as a Distribution System

Water flows, and as it does it distributes pollutants, nutrients, plants, and animals. Although Massachusetts Bay is a clean body of water, many sources of pollution may affect the Bank. Most of the pollution arises from land sources—runoff, rivers, sewage outfalls—and the atmosphere. There are also marine pollutants: oils and toxic chemicals from ships, debris from trash disposal at sea, and various chemicals disposed of at ocean dumpsites. Generally, the pollution of the coastal environment is tightly controlled by government agencies. However, the distribution of pollutants via air and currents means that pollution generated far from Stellwagen Bank may disrupt the balances of the Stellwagen ecosystem, making control of the pollutants much more difficult.

Nutrients that act as fertilizers for the plants of the Bank are also brought to the Bank by currents. The

INDUSTRIAL WASTES
AND TOXIC
CONTAMINANTS

SEWAGE AND
GARBAGE

AIRBORNE
CONTAMINANTS

PESTICIDES,
FERTILIZER, AND
ANIMAL WASTE
RUNOFF

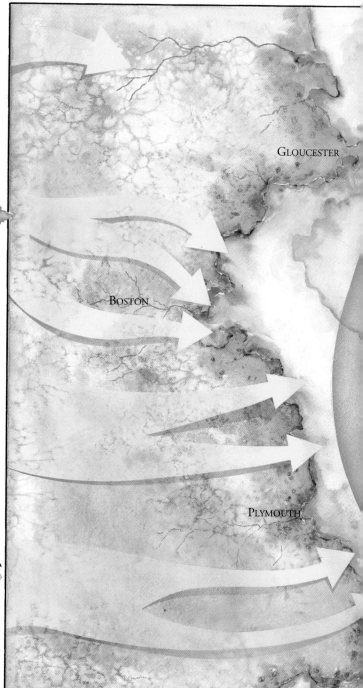

GLOUCESTER

BOSTON

PLYMOUTH

*Water moving at about one to two knots sweeps south from the Gulf of
Maine and carries cold, nutrient-rich water into the Stellwagen Bank
region (blue arrows). On its journey south, the water quality is slowly
changed by land-based and airborne pollutants (yellow arrows), as well*

36

TOXIC DUMPING
AT SEA

GARBAGE, CHEMICALS,
PLASTICS
DUMPED AT SEA

STELLWAGEN
BANK

PROVINCETOWN

*as marine pollutants (gray arrows). Tides and local currents (turquoise
arrows) also influence the Bank's system on a smaller scale as they
transport nutrients and thereby affect the distribution of marine
animals.* (E. Paul Oberlander)

37

UPWELLING AND SLICKS

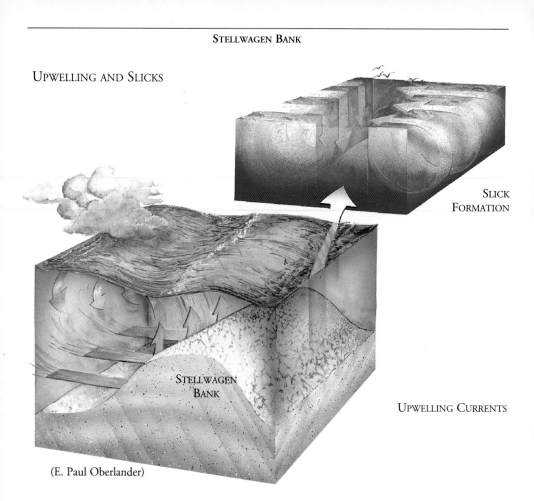

SLICK
FORMATION

STELLWAGEN
BANK

UPWELLING CURRENTS

(E. Paul Oberlander)

Stellwagen Bank rises abruptly from the bottom of Massachusetts Bay, forming an extensive underwater plateau. One effect of this geologic configuration is upwelling.

Upwelling occurs when underwater currents and changing tides are deflected by the steep walls of the Bank, bringing nutrient-laden water up from the depths toward the surface. In the shallower waters over the Bank, the phytoplankton—microscopic plants—multiply rapidly, taking advantage of the sunlight, warmer water temperatures, and inflowing nutrients. Zooplankton—tiny marine animals—rise in the water to eat the burgeoning population of phytoplankton. Fish that feed on the abundant zooplankton are in turn eaten by other fish, seabirds, and whales. All members of the food web thus benefit from the upwelling that begins the cycle.

Slicks occur in areas where two currents meet. The downward circulating water produces a calm, slick area on the surface in which organic matter concentrates. Fish and sea birds often congregate over slicks, taking advantage of these productive feeding areas.

sources of nutrients are many, and the processes that bring them to the Bank are complex. Nutrients are generated at sea by the decomposition of plants and animals. Upwelling currents bring these nutrients to the surface. Nutrients generated on the land, in coastal estuaries, and in productive salt marshes contribute to the near-shore richness. Tidal currents then flush the nutrients from estuarine habitats out to Stellwagen Bank. These fertilizers are essential to the Bank ecosystem, as are the processes that generate them (decomposition), the balances that control their concentrations, and the distribution processes (currents) that make the fertilizers available to the plants.

For some species, such as barnacles and clams, currents are essential to their survival. Such species release their microscopic young to drift where the currents will take them. This passive dispersion permits them to colonize new habitats after they settle to the bottom to begin their sedentary life. Even larval stages of commercially important species, such as flounder and lobsters, depend on currents to disperse their offspring to favorable habitats. Without this larval dispersion, some species would be trapped in restricted areas of the bottom, unable to pioneer new habitats that periodically become available.

The Vital Process: Seasonal Change

From May through September, microscopic plants known as phytoplankton capture the energy of sunlight through photosynthesis. As they die or are consumed, they sink toward the bottom where they break down further into inorganic nutrients.

During this time of the year, the water at the surface of the Bank is warmed by the sun to as much as 68°F (20°C). Because this warm water is slightly lighter than the colder and more dense deep water—around 50°F (10°C)—it lies as a layer on the surface. Roughly 16.4 feet (5 meters) beneath the surface is the thermocline, the boundary between the warm and cold layers. (The exact depth depends on the amount of mixing by the waves.) Because of water's density differences and the

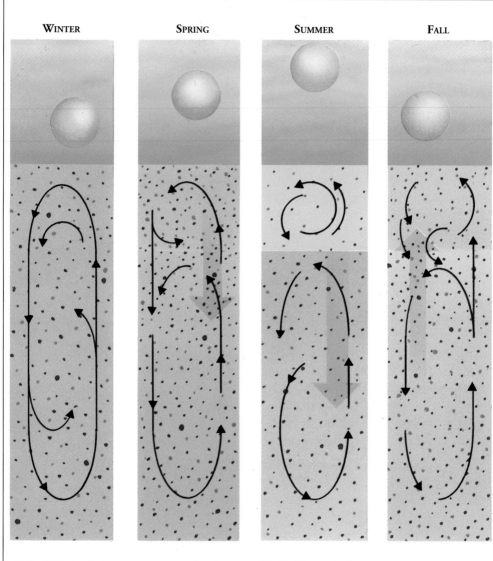

| WINTER | SPRING | SUMMER | FALL |

(E. Paul Oberlander)

Small arrows (black): Water circulation or mixing
Large arrows (blue): Direction of nutrient flow
Green dots: Phytoplankton
Red dots: Nutrients

THE SEASONAL OVERTURN OF PLANKTON

Just as life on land is ultimately dependent on the sun for its existence, so it is in the sea. The seasonal influence of light, temperature, and currents govern the distribution of plankton in the surface layers of the water.

Winter. The sun's rays are relatively weak. Chilling winds and waves generate a circulation throughout the water column, bringing rich nutrient stores to the near-surface layers. The sea becomes uniformly cold and enriched with nutrients, but the low light level and violent mixing prevent prolific phytoplankton growth.

Spring. As the sun gets higher and more light is available, the water warms and phytoplankton in the surface layers grow rapidly, taking advantage of the abundant nutrients. The phytoplankton blooms turn the blue-gray winter waters green as vast areas are transformed into lush "pastures."

As spring progresses, zooplankton populations also increase rapidly. By late spring, the phytoplankton bloom consumes the surface supply of nutrients in the sunlit layers and grazing zooplankton reduce the density of the phytoplankton. Mixing subsides, and a temperature boundary (thermocline) develops between the warm, less dense surface water and the cooler water below.

Summer. By summer, the pace slackens. The thermocline prevents circulation between the two water layers. Nutrient supply is low near the surface, and phytoplankton and zooplankton abundance is reduced.

Fall. As the autumn winds blow and solar energy declines, the thermocline breaks down. Waters begin to mix again, and nutrients flood into the well-lit upper layers. With nutrients again available, a fall crop of phytoplankton has a brief period of abundance before winter sets in and the upwelling cycle begins anew.

stability of the layers, the thermocline acts as a boundary, and the water in the two layers does not mix. However, some of the nutrient-rich material produced by photosynthesis in the warm, sunlit layer does rain down into the deeper layer. These nutrients thus become concentrated in the bottom water and unavailable to the plants, which need to be near the surface, in bright sun, to photosynthesize. Returning nutrients to the surface, where they can be used by phytoplankton, is therefore a critical revitalizing process.

During the summer upwelling, currents in turbulent areas along the margins of the Bank help replenish the surface with nutrients. Strong storms also contribute to mixing of the waters. Perhaps the most important period of nutrient replenishment occurs during the fall. As the air temperature and sunlight decrease, the surface layer cools and the thermocline becomes less stable. In time, the mixing of storm waves and the decrease in difference between the surface and bottom water temperatures leads to an "overturn."

During the fall overturn, and all through the cold months of the year, nutrient-rich bottom water freely mixes to the surface. During this season, due to low light and temperature, phytoplankton photosynthesis is slow, but as spring progresses and sunlight becomes stronger, the concentrated nutrients now at the surface support a plankton "bloom" that turns some parts of the Stellwagen system a dark grass-green. As this cycle continues, the thermocline forms again and the nutrients are lost once more to the surface layer until mixing returns them to the surface to be revitalized.

Balance and Connections

As in all environments, the complicated relationships among the plants and animals of the Stellwagen Bank system are most easily seen as connections between predators and prey, as critical links in a grand and dynamic food web. Every connection is vital; each living part of the system reacts to all of its connections. Therefore, a change in the number, behavior, physiological condition, or location of any organism will affect,

Diatoms. Each diatom is an independent plant, a miniature chemical factory that uses solar energy to convert inorganic substances into the materials vital to life. Diatoms are part of the indispensable first link in almost every food chain in the sea; many marine animals depend directly or indirectly upon diatoms for nourishment.

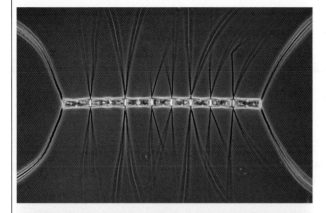

Diatoms may occur as single individuals or as linked chains of varying lengths, like these eight Chaetoceros affins *diatoms. Each cell has four spines that help it stay afloat. (Length about 0.2 mm.)* (Paul Hargraves)

The cells of this corkscrew-shaped diatom, Chaetoceros debilis, *are linked by fusion of their silica spines. (Length 0.2 mm.)* (Paul Hargraves)

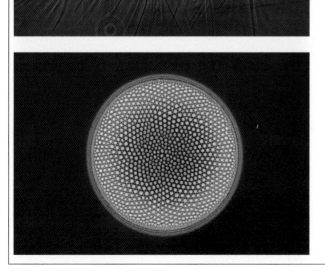

Like a jeweled pillbox, the intricately sculptured cell of Coscinodiscus *is formed of two lidlike structures that fit together like a little box; hence the name diatom, meaning "cut in two." (Length about 0.1 mm.)* (Paul Hargraves)

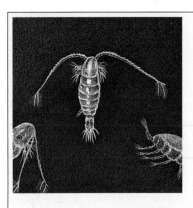

Copepods, minute crustaceans, are one of the main links in the food chain between plant matter and the rest of the life in the sea. Copepods eat diatoms, large copepods eat smaller ones, and members of almost every other invertebrate group are eating ceaselessly and awaiting their turn to be eaten by some other predator. (Tessa Morgan)

*A snail larva (*Gastropod veliger*) drifts as a member of the zooplankton only during the early stages of its life. It grazes on phytoplankton until it settles on the sea floor as a tiny periwinkle. (Length about 0.5 mm.)* (Paul Hargraves)

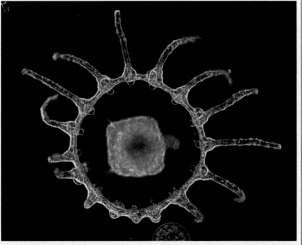

Like so many animals, the jellyfish passes through a planktonic stage before changing into the adult. This young medusa measures about one millimeter. (Paul Hargraves)

directly or indirectly, every other organism. The sensitive relationship among these elements leads to a condition of dynamic equilibrium in which continual change is the essence of a system that only appears changeless.

The Fuel for the System

The Stellwagen Bank system is fueled by the richest source of food on earth: plankton. The plankton drifts, invisible to the casual observer. It is a whole ecosystem on a miniature scale, with millions of microscopic plants and animals in each gallon (3.8 liters) of sea water. In a microscopic food web of their own, the plankton carry on the complex interactions typical of all food webs. Plankton might be only a passing curiosity but for the fact that many different kinds of planktonic plants (some fifty species) and animals (perhaps seventy-five species) directly or indirectly feed every organism that lives on, in, or over the Bank.

The plants, or phytoplankton, need only clean water, nutrients transported by currents, and sunlight to begin the process of photosynthesis. It is phytoplankton, the grass of the sea, that capture the energy of sunlight through growth and reproduction and thereby make the energy of sunlight available to the larger plant-eating animals, the zooplankton. Then, through the food web, plankton provide fuel to the larger organisms that thrive at the bottom and mid-water levels of the system. Many species of plankton-feeding marine animals, such as herring, shellfish, and worms, play an essential role in indirectly connecting the rich and abundant plankton to other parts of the food web of Stellwagen Bank.

Nearly all the life in the sea depends on plankton or on food web connections to plankton. But the unseen planktonic system is not only the food source of the sea; it is also its nursery. The planktonic environment supports nearly all of the young stages of fish and shellfish in the ocean. So it is that each year the rich resources of Stellwagen Bank—cod, flounder, sea clams, and lobsters —release billions upon billions of tiny, drifting larvae to take up a temporary existence in the plankton environment, feeding, interacting, and maturing there.

Zooplankton   Phytoplankton

(E. Paul Oberlander)

SURFACE WATERS

MID-WATER

BOTTOM WATERS

The Food Web

Although it is convenient for us to divide the water column into layers, as shown, the interactions between the organisms of the Bank cross all arbitrary boundaries and form an extraordinarily complex and tightly interdependent web of consumers.

Phytoplankton—drifting microscopic plants such as diatoms and dinoflagellates—are primary producers. They use the sun's energy to convert inorganic substances into the materials vital to animal life: carbohydrates, fats, proteins, and vitamins.

CONTINUED ON PAGE 48

47

Zooplankton. The legions of zooplankton—the tiny animals that feed on the phytoplankton—include tiny crustaceans such as copepods, winged snails (pteropods), jellyfish, and fish larvae. Zooplankton are consumed by fish, sea birds, and filter feeders such as the North Atlantic right whale.

Surface Waters. A microscopic world of plant and animal plankton flourishes in the surface waters. As plankton die, they join the slow rain of other dead animals, plants, and wastes that drift gradually to the bottom of the sea. Some of this detritus is consumed as it falls to the bottom.

Activity in the surface waters is intense. Here, marine mammals and sea turtles—the air breathers—are most active. Sea birds and other predators depend on foraging fishes, such as sand lance and herring, to make their living.

Mid-Water is a place with few boundaries. Predators move between the surface and bottom waters to feed on the abundant organisms found in the mid-waters.

Much of the Bank's sinking organic material is consumed here. Large schools of herring and squid are found. Gelatinous siphonophores and jellyfish drift with the currents. Humpback whales and bluefin tuna drive schools of fish up toward the surface to catch them. With the exception of these interactions, the mid-water activity remains unseen from the surface.

Benthos, or Bottom Waters. A variety of animals move about the bottom feeding upon other animals and detritus. Sculpins, lobsters, and other scavengers feed on bits of food found on the sea floor. Groundfish such as codfish, pollock, and flounder alternately feed on the bottom or just above it.

Sea anemones, sponges, and tunicates populate rock faces. Clams and scallops filter the omnipresent plankton that have drifted down from the surface waters above. Upwelling currents carry eggs and tiny larvae of bottom-dwelling animals to the surface waters, where abundant food will help them develop during the early stages of their life cycle.

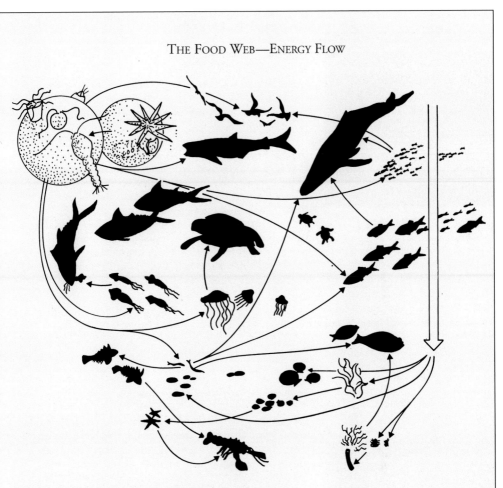

The arrows indicate the direction of food energy flow from its source—the sun, to plants (producers), and then to the various levels of consumer organisms. This simplified version of the Stellwagen Bank food web does not include all the food sources for every animal.

Animals are not drawn to scale.

*Boring sponges (*Cliona celata*) riddle mollusk shells. As the sponge grows, it secretes sulfuric acid, which weakens and dissolves the host's shell to the point of disintegration. Boring sponges attach themselves to empty shells as well as occupied ones, and are a significant factor in helping to break down accumulations of shells on the sea floor. They can be devastating to oyster beds, however.* (Herb Segars)

INVERTEBRATES OF STELLWAGEN BANK

Sponges, jellyfish, snails, clams, squid, shrimp, lobster and sea stars are all invertebrates—animals without the internal support of a backbone. Some of these animals are anchored to the bottom where they feed on what currents bring them. Others roam the bottom in search of food (one notable exception, the squid, moves throughout the mid-waters and is not bottom-dwelling).

Sponges come in a variety of colors and shapes: tiny vases, long fingers, thick branches, flattened encrustations, or huge pipelike masses. They attach themselves to rocks, shells, or pilings. The simplest of the multicelled animals, they have neither organs nor organ systems.

Fixed permanently to one spot, sponges feed by filtering seawater through a network of canals in their bodies. The water is drawn into the sponge through minute pores called *ostia*. Inside, specialized collar cells filter out minute planktonic organisms and bits of detritus.

Cnidarians: Corals, Hydroids, Anemones, Jellyfish, and Siphonophores. The cnidarians have two basic body forms: the polyp and the medusa. In cnidarians, one opening into the gut serves as both a mouth and an exit of waste, eggs, and sperm.

The flowerlike polyps, represented by hydroids, corals, and sea anemones, are sessile, or stationary. The anemone's body consists of a fleshy column—one end of its tubular body has a slitlike mouth surrounded by tentacles while the other end is attached to the substrate.

The bell-shaped medusas—typified by jellyfish and siphonophores—are planktonic and capable of swimming, though on a larger scale, their movements are influenced by tides, currents, and winds.

*The fleshy, club-shaped branches of branching soft coral (*Gersemia rubiformis*) grow to a height of six inches or more. Soft corals do not have the rigid support provided by the calcium carbonate skeletons of reef-building corals.* (Wes Pratt)

What looks like a bouquet of tiny pink flowers is actually a colony of pink-hearted hydroids (Tubularia crocea). The stems are about 1.2 inches (3 cm) long and the blossom is 0.39 inch (1 cm) across. Each "blossom" is an animal, a polyp, shaped like an inverted cone surrounded by tentacles. The grapelike clusters in the center of the whorl of tentacles are the reproductive organs. (Herb Segars)

The chrysanthemum-like northern red anemone (Urticina felina) is a carnivorous animal capable of catching, killing, and digesting prey as large as fish. The hundred pinkish tentacles that ring the anemone's mouth are equipped with nematocysts, specialized capsules that contain explosive cells. When the anemone is disturbed, the nematocysts discharge poisonous threads that stun and capture prey. The anemone's tentacles then retract, pulling the food into the mouth, which is at the center of the oral disk. When threatened, sea anemones contract into leathery lumps to protect themselves. (Jon Witman)

 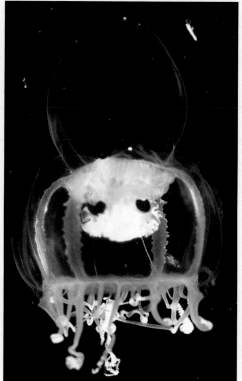

*A tiny gas float (on top) filled with carbon monoxide keeps this siphono- phore (*Physophora hydrostatica) *afloat. This siphonophore propels itself with six pairs of vase-shaped swimming bells, which contract rhythmically. It captures prey with its opalescent pink tentacles, around which are tiny stinging cells.* (Richard Harbison)

Jellyfish capture their prey with specialized stinging cells that contain poison-filled sacs, called nematocysts. Inside each nematocyst is a tightly coiled dart that uncoils explosively when stimulated and injects venom into the prey. (Richard Harbison)

Ctenophores, or Comb Jellies. Often mistaken for jellyfish, ctenophores are fragile, transparent, and gelatinous. Water makes up more than 95 percent of their body weight. Unlike jellyfish, comb jellies do not sting. These seemingly innocuous animals are voracious predators nonetheless, feeding on a variety of tiny crustaceans and fish.

Most comb jellies have eight rows of comblike plates radiating like longitudinal lines on a globe, running from the mouth on top to the bottom. The comb plates are covered with fine hairs, or cilia, which create a current that moves the animal through the water. They are weak swimmers, and rely on currents and tides to move them about.

Comb jellies are hermaphrodites, with both male and female gonads located along the colorful plates, eggs on one side and sperm on the other. Eggs and sperm are released into the water, where fertilization takes place. Larvae hatch within twenty-four hours.

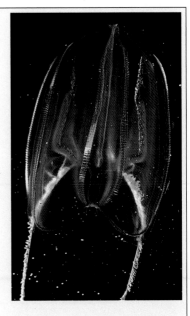

*The long pink tentacles of the Arctic sea gooseberry (*Mertensia ovum*) are covered with a sticky substance that catches small swimming crustaceans. This species of comb jelly reaches a length of two inches (5 cm). (Richard Harbison)*

Marine Worms. Some marine worms are nomadic explorers, crawling among stones and shells and algae communities. Others dwell in parchment tubes woven of bits of shell, seaweed, and other debris. Some filter food from the seawater, while others are adept predators that feed on other soft-bodied creatures.

*Often called the ice-cream-cone worm, the trumpet worm (*Pectinari goudi*) is a master mason. It builds a conical tube, one sand grain thick, selected from surrounding sediments and then cemented together by mucus. (Wes Pratt)*

53

Bryozoans. Resembling feathery seaweeds, mosslike mats, or even embroidered cloth, bryozoan colonies can take a variety of forms. The individual organism lies within a body case that may be gelatinous, rubbery, or chitinous (like the tough exoskeleton of crabs and lobsters).

*Colonies of spiral tufted bryozoans (*Bugula turrita*) may grow to almost one foot (30 cm) in height. The yellow branches are made up of hundreds of minute animals, each less than .03 inch (1 mm) in size. Each individual, called a zooid, captures tiny crustaceans with its tentacles.* (Wes Pratt)

Brachiopods. Although a brachiopod shell is made up of two valves, like that of a bivalve mollusk, its valves are oriented upper and lower rather than left and right. Another difference from mollusks is the fleshy stalk that anchors the brachiopod to the substrate.

*The teardrop-shaped northern lamp shell (*Terebratulina septentrinonalis*) is about one and a quarter inches (3.2 cm) long. The lacy filaments between the shells, called lophophores, trap food particles. The bowl-like lower shell is reminiscent of an ancient Roman lamp, giving it the common name of lamp shell.* (Wes Pratt)

Mollusks. Since prehistoric times, humans have eaten mollusks, making them more familiar to most people than any other invertebrate group. Mollusks include clams, whelks, squid, scallops, mussels, and some not so familiar creatures.

Several distinctive features are found only in mollusks. One is the mantle, a tissue that completely covers—and secretes the calcium shell of— snails, clams, and scallops. (In squid, the mantle is hidden inside, and it is found only in the embryonic stage of sea slugs.) Another mollusk feature is the radula, the animal's flexible, rasplike tongue, which is used to obtain food. And finally, there is the foot, the muscular structure on which some mollusks, such as whelks and snails, creep along the seabed. (The foot has become specialized to form tentacles in squid.)

Nudibranchs are sea slugs, mollusks that have no shell. The red-gilled nudibranch (Coryphella rufi- branchialis) *has two pairs of tentacles, and its back is covered with a hundred slender fingerlike projections. Each projection contains an extension of the gut. When the nudibranch feeds on a hydroid, it is not deterred by the hydroid's stinging cells. In fact, it incorporates these cells into its skin for its own defense.* (Wes Pratt)

Left: *Looking like a skein of yarn, this mass of white eggs from a red-gilled nudibranch may contain a million eggs.* (Kevin McCarthy)

*This long-finned squid (*Loligo pealei) *has just nabbed a flounder with its tentacles. Squid are another type of shell-less mollusk. A squid moves by jet propulsion, drawing water into the mantle cavity through slits behind the head and expelling it forcefully through a siphon below the neck. It can aim its siphon either forward or backward, choosing its preferred direction. They occur in schools of hundreds and are eaten by sea bass, bluefish, mackerel, and pilot whales.* (Kevin McCarthy)

55

This fingerlike gelatinous mass contains encapsulated yolky eggs that will hatch as miniature adult squid. The egg clusters are deposited on algae or other substrate, often being cemented in place. Each capsule is two inches (5 cm) long and holds up to 200 eggs. (Sue and David Millhouser)

Arthropods. The most obvious characteristics of arthropods —crabs, lobsters, shrimp, and their relatives—are their segmented, armorlike exoskeleton and their jointed legs. The exoskeleton cannot expand; to grow, crabs and lobsters have to molt periodically and grow a new, larger exoskeleton.

Acadian hermit crab, Pagurus acadianus. Hermit crabs have the peculiar habit of occupying empty gastropod shells. Like all crustaceans, they shed their chitinous shell to grow. As they do so, they must also replace the borrowed gastropod shell that protects their soft, shell-less abdomen and find a bigger one— searching out an ideal fit. (Ed Lyman)

Resembling a praying mantis, but less than an inch long (26 mm), the long-horned skeleton shrimp (Aeginella longicornis) is the largest skeleton shrimp in American Atlantic waters. (Wes Pratt)

The long-legged lentil sea spider (Anopodactylus lentus) feeds on hydroids. Its reddish-purple color is due to a dark red pigment in its blood. (Wes Pratt)

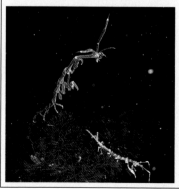

Echinoderms. Starfish, brittle stars, sea urchins, sea cucumbers, and sand dollars are all echinoderms. Their most apparent common feature is their spokelike design, or radial symmetry. The body is almost always arranged in five parts, or multiples thereof. They also have a spiny skin, or modifications on that theme, hence their Latin name *echinoderm*, which means "hedgehog skin." Finally, they have an internal water vascular system which powers their flexible suction-cup "tube feet" and provides their means of locomotion.

The northern basket star (Gorgono-cephalus arcticus) a highly mobile echinoderm, lacks the grooves and tube feet of sea stars. Its five many-branched arms (12 to 18 inches, or 30 to 45 cm, long) create a trap eighteen inches across. Outspread, the arms sweep the currents for zooplankton and tiny fish. The tips of each branchlet seize the prey. This basket star has just begun to feed. Eventually, when all the branchlets are full of miniature knots, the basket star will curl the whole arm to its mouth and ingest its bounty. (Jon Witman)

This many-armed purple sunstar (Solaster endeca) may have up to fourteen flexible arms. Sea stars can regenerate lost arms, a process called autonomy. The damaged arm is shed, and regeneration of a new arm begins. (Note the shortened arm at upper left.) The sunstar preys mainly on sea cucumbers and other sea stars. (Jon Witman)

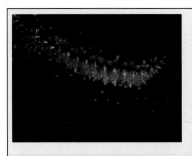

Above: *Starfish get around on their tube feet. Each water-filled tube is extended as water is pumped out of it. Suckers on the ends of the tubes grasp the surface. Muscles then pull water back in, causing the tubes to swell and shorten, which draws the animal up to where the suckers are fastened.* (Ed Lyman)

Right: *The strikingly colored scarlet psolus sea cucumber (*Psolus fabricii*) has ten tentacles, or arms. One arm (right) is stuffing food into the sea cucumber's mouth, while the others are extended to snare more prey.* (Wes Pratt)

Tunicates. Tunicates are primitive relatives of vertebrates. During their larval development, they possess a notochord, a stiffened rodlike support. Their name comes from the tough external covering, or tunic, that encloses the body of these animals. Tunicates, or sea squirts, are sedentary animals and can easily be mistaken for sponges. Like sponges, sea squirts filter sea water for plankton and detritus.

Stalked Ascidian, Boltenia ovifera. *The body of a sea squirt looks like a shrunken carrot with two conspicuous spouts or siphons—one opening through which water and plankton enter and another through which wastes are eliminated. Prodding a sea squirt usually provokes the ejection of a short spurt of water, hence their common name.* (Kevin McCarthy)

SEA BIRDS

MASTERS OF WIND AND WATER, sea birds may amuse and baffle both casual observers and seasoned birdwatchers. Our knowledge of sea birds' lives is, at best, fragmentary. Until recently, much of what we know about them has been gathered from their behavior on their breeding grounds. Stellwagen Bank, however, affords the unique opportunity to study sea birds at sea.

Through the years, sea birds and their biology have been shrouded in myth and legend. For centuries, however, sailors have relied on sea bird flight lines to help them find land. Similarly, generations of fishermen have gleaned information about fish stocks by noting the behavior and occurrence of sea birds. Today, scientists use them as barometers for food abundance, the natural cyclic changes within the habitat, and the health of the marine ecosystem.

The mature northern gannet is dazzling white except for a yellowish tinge on the head and jet black wingtips. (Robert Abrams)

*An uncommon visitor to Stellwagen Bank, an Iceland gull (*Larus glaucoides*) snares a fish.* (VIREO)

Sea birds are an important resource in the Sanctuary in that they coexist with, and depend upon, a variety of other marine organisms. Their activities vary with the time of day, the weather, the season, their reproductive stage and behavior, and the activities of other marine creatures, such as fish and plankton.

Sea birds have effectively shaped their feeding methods to garner the varied resources of the sea. Each sea bird species is identified by its own distinctive characteristics that demonstrate its unique adaptations to a marine existence. Although correctly identifying species is important, perhaps the more valuable lesson is to gain an understanding of how these birds use their marine habitat.

Nearly forty species of marine birds occur regularly within the Sanctuary's boundaries. However, the abundance and distribution of the different species change constantly from season to season, and often from year to year. Some species are strictly pelagic and spend more than half of their lives on the open ocean, coming ashore only to breed. The Sanctuary is an important seasonal gathering point in their journeys, which, for some species, take them from one hemisphere to another.

For most of us, the mere thought of being alone under the vast circle of sky, surrounded by heaving, racing ocean swells, is enough to sicken the heart. But to the sea birds that spend most of their life on the sea, this is home.

The Tubenoses

Pelagic bird species are long-lived, with an average life span of up to twenty years. The largest group of truly pelagic birds is the order Procellariiformes (from the Latin *procella,* "pertaining to storms"), which contains storm petrels, shearwaters, and fulmars. Collectively, the members of this order are called "tubenoses," referring to their noticeable external, tubelike nostrils, which aid in the excretion of salt and the detection of odors.

Tubenoses spend a relatively brief time on land, where they breed in huge colonies on isolated islands. Nearly all species either excavate nesting burrows with their webbed feet or place their single egg in rock

With stiff-set wings, the northern fulmar glides across mirror-smooth water. This dark phase bird is not as common in the Sanctuary as light phase individuals. (VIREO)

crevices or on ledges, inaccessible to all but winged predators. Incubation and fledgling periods are protracted, lasting two to five months depending on the species. Parents feed their chicks a meal of regurgitated oil or partially digested food, but as the chick matures, parental visits become less frequent. Eventually, parents abandon their chicks.

At this point, the youngsters launch themselves into their marine world. An immature bird may remain at sea for up to ten years before it returns to land to breed for the first time. Because of their strong nest-site fidelity, sea birds often breed with the same mate year after year, although they generally do not remain together outside the breeding season.

Wilson's Storm Petrel

Among the smallest of the sea birds that frequent Stellwagen Bank is the sooty-colored Wilson's storm petrel (*Oceanites oceanicus*). Hydrobatidae, the scientific name of the family to which all storm petrels belong, comes from the Greek words meaning "one who treads on water." At times, especially when feeding, storm petrels patter their feet on the surface of the water. This propensity for "walking on water" undoubtedly inspired the name "petrel," which links them to St. Peter, who is said to have walked on the Sea of Galilee. In Provincetown they are called "Jesus birds" for the same reason.

Rafts of these small birds, also nicknamed "Mother Carey's Chickens" by mariners (a corruption from *Mater Cara,* the Blessed Virgin), often huddle together on the

The Wilson's storm petrel's striking white rump patch contrasts sharply with its dark plumage. With wings held high, it patters its long, spindly legs on the surface of the water. (Wayne Petersen)

A group of Wilson's storm petrels, fluttering just above the sea's swell, look like tiny storm-tossed kites at the mercy of wind and wave. (Tessa Morgan)

The greater shearwater is brown above and white beneath, with a white collar, a dark cap, and a narrow horseshoe-shaped rump patch. (Tessa Morgan)

ocean's swells. In windy weather, they skim above the waves on set wings, periodically using both feet to spring along the surface in a series of hops. At other times, they seem to skip restlessly over the swells, stopping occasionally to dip their bills into the water to pick up whatever oily matter or tiny organisms they find on the surface. These organisms typically include a combination of protozoa, bacteria, microalgae, fish eggs, larval fish, and the larvae of crustaceans.

During the northern winter, which is the southern hemisphere's summer, Wilson's storm petrels nest on islands off the tip of South America and around the perimeter of the Antarctic subcontinent. Some ornithologists consider the Wilson's storm petrel to be the most abundant bird in the world, with a global population estimated in the hundreds of millions.

Shearwaters

Shearwaters are named for their gliding flight, which often scales these slim-winged sea birds just above the wave tops. In windy weather, a series of rapid wing beats gives shearwaters momentum for a prolonged glide upon stiffly extended wings. Tipping from side to side to trim sail, the birds effortlessly ride updrafts between the waves, occasionally skimming low into the wave's trough, only to reappear beyond the next crest. In calm

weather, they often gather in small groups amid resting flocks of gulls.

Shearwaters are seen with some regularity in the Sanctuary during the summer. Most common are greater shearwaters (*Puffinus gravis*) and sooty shearwaters (*Puffinus griseus*). Manx shearwaters (*Puffinus puffinus*) are occasionally seen, and in some years, Cory's shearwaters (*Calonectris diomedea*) appear in late summer. The relative distribution of each species is dependent on food availability and water temperature. Like Wilson's storm petrels, greater and sooty shearwaters enjoy a perpetual summer since they breed in the southern hemisphere during the northern winter.

Schools of fish will quickly attract a crowd of these offshore wanderers. At times, shearwaters in full flight will make shallow dives for fish, while on other occasions they feed from the surface. Much of their feeding takes place in the twilight hours when squid, small crustaceans, and certain small fish are most prevalent near the water's surface. Fishermen familiar with the shearwaters' greedy practice of noisily squabbling over floating offal or oily fish wastes left by fishing vessels have nicknamed them "hags" or "haglets."

Northern Fulmar

The northern fulmar (*Fulmarus glacialis*) is easily mistaken for a herring gull due to its variable colors, which range from a uniform smoky-gray to a creamy-white. However, the fulmar's tubular nostrils, stout yellow bill, large dark eyes, and stiff-winged flight immediately separate it from the more familiar gull.

Fulmar literally means "foul mew" or "gull" in Ice-

Left: *To take off, a greater shearwater faces into the wind and runs vigorously over the water until airborne, leaving a wake of splashes a yard or two apart.* (Robert Abrams)

Right: *The sooty shearwater is a uniformly dark bird with pale wing linings.* (VIREO)

Feeding far out at sea, manx shearwaters take small crustaceans and fish. They are seen resting on the sea less frequently than sooty and greater shearwaters. (Wayne Petersen)

The northern fulmar's cold, dark eye and clean appearance may explain one of its colloquial names: marblehead. Light phase birds such as this one are largely white with a pale gray back and "windows" on the wings. (Robert Abrams)

landic, and refers to the bird's defensive habit of regurgitating a musky smelling oil when threatened. Speculation is rife as to the use of the oil. This unusual substance, which is common to all tubenoses, typically gives them and their nesting sites a distinctive odor. Fulmar oil was once commercially collected on the Scottish island of St. Kilda, where it was used as fuel for oil lamps and in certain medicines. Interestingly, this stomach oil is similar in composition to the spermaceti found in the head of the sperm whale.

Historically, these audacious birds were seen following northern whaling ships, often swarming in the oily wake as they picked up scraps of blubber thrown overboard. Fulmars are opportunistic feeders that regularly consume a varied diet of zooplankton, fish, squid, and gurry from fishing vessels, most of which they seize from the surface of the water. Like the shearwaters, they have prodigious appetites and occasionally gorge themselves to the point where they seem loath to rise off the water, even when disturbed.

Slow to mature, fulmars are probably at least six years old before they begin breeding. They nest in the Arctic during the summer and only range south to our waters during the nonbreeding seasons. Here, they appear on the offshore fishing banks in late autumn when, with stiff-set wings, they brave strong winter gales. Banking and gliding just above the waves, they alight periodically on the surface with an ungraceful splash.

THE SALT SOLUTION

As any sailor will readily point out, a person who drinks seawater will become even more thirsty. To prevent dehydration, the salt contained in the water must be excreted by the kidneys, thus depleting the body's fluid level even further. Most air-breathing vertebrates are unable to tolerate drinking seawater, but some are less restricted than others.

Sea birds, whales, seals, and sea turtles, whose ancestors dwelt on land, now find their homes often hundreds of miles from any source of fresh water, yet

all these animals rely on fresh water to live. Indeed, they must limit the concentration of salt in their body fluids and blood to about one percent—less than a third of the salt concentration in seawater. If they drink seawater, they must find some means to get rid of excess salt, but if they do not drink seawater, where do they obtain the water their body tissues require?

It has long been known that sea birds drink seawater with impunity. Elegantly specialized salt glands enable marine birds to meet their fluid needs by drinking seawater and then removing excess salt from the bloodstream. To do this, most sea birds possess salt glands, which are located behind the eyes and connected to the nostrils. These glands secrete a concentrated salt solution through the ducts of the nasal cavities. In most species, the salty fluid flows out through the nostrils and drips from the tip of their bills, which explains why sea birds are often seen shaking their heads —they are actually ridding themselves of the salty droplets. Storm petrels have evolved a curious "water-pistol" mechanism to rid themselves of excess salt while in flight. Their peculiar tube-shaped nostrils, which are situated along the top of the bill near the base, can shoot the salt solution a distance of two feet (61 cm) when the bird is disturbed.

Like the Mock Turtle in *Alice's Adventures in Wonderland,* sea turtles also weep. Research on loggerhead sea turtles has demonstrated that turtle tears come from a large gland behind the eyeball that is strikingly similar to the salt glands in sea birds. It is plausible that the sea turtle's copious tears also assist in salt elimination.

Investigations of seals and dolphins indicate that marine mammals remove salt from their systems in a more conventional manner. Apparently these animals do not drink seawater, but satisfy their need for water with the fluids contained in their diet of plankton, fish, squid, or shellfish. Physiological studies suggest that their kidneys are able to dispose of the concentrated salt solution without troublesome effects.

A Wilson's storm petrel's tubular nostrils "fire" salty droplets, excreting excess salt that accumulates in its body's tissues. Sea turtles, such as the leatherback shown here, excrete excess salt through their copious "tears." (Tessa Morgan; Sarah Landry)

65

In sharp contrast to the mostly white adult, the juvenile northern gannet is dark brown, speckled with white—a plumage phase it will keep for the first year of its life. (Robert Abrams)

*A circumpolar breeding species, the Sabine's gull (*Xema sabini*) nests in the Canadian Arctic in North America and is a rare visitor to Stellwagen Bank.* (Robert Abrams)

Gannets

Many sea birds, including gannets and terns, are expert plunge divers. To watch them plunge-dive for food is a thrilling sight, especially when many birds hit the water in rapid succession. From a height of 43 feet (13 meters) or more, and with such force that their torpedo-shaped bodies disappear entirely beneath the surface, gannets dive in pursuit of small fish. With partially closed wings, the birds make a half twist as they progress downward, then finally close their wings before the moment of impact. They occasionally plunge to depths of more than 10 feet (3 meters), and the dive's impact may send a shower of spray 10 feet (3 meters) into the air. To cushion the shock of hitting the water, gannets have a built-in system of inflatable air sacs beneath the skin of their heads and necks. After surfacing from a dive, they rest momentarily on the surface, easily swallowing whole fish with the aid of their distensible throat.

The northern gannet (*Morus bassanus*) is the largest sea bird in the North Atlantic. Its name comes from the Old English *gan* meaning "gander" or "gooselike." In the mid-nineteenth century, gannet populations were drastically reduced, due to human exploitation of their Canadian breeding colonies. Gannets are most numerous on Stellwagen Bank when they are migrating in early spring and late fall. Steady, vigorous wing strokes, alternated with periods of gliding, characterize the northern gannets' flight pattern.

Gulls and Terns

Approximately ten species of gulls and terns regularly frequent Stellwagen Bank. While both groups are gregarious by nature, the gulls are generally larger than their allies, the more dainty and streamlined terns. Gulls and terns are easily distinguished from one another. The upper mandible of a gull's bill is ridged and slightly hooked at the end, whereas terns have pointed bills that are virtually straight. When searching for food, gulls usually fly with their bill held nearly parallel with the water, while terns often point their bills downward. Although both gulls and terns are web-footed and capable of swim-

66

PLUNGE DIVING

*The gannet hunts by heading upwind, fixing its binocular
gaze at the water. Spotting an individual fish, it adjusts the
angle and position of its body as it corkscrews down before
taking the final plunge.*

(Illustration by Sarah Landry, based on
photographs by Vincent Guadazno.)

Most species of terns, or sea swallows, are easily identified by their slender pointed wings, small body, and deeply forked tail. In flight, the common tern's bill points downward as the bird searches for fish. (Tessa Morgan)

ming, gulls demonstrate minimal diving skills and, consequently, are scavengers that prey chiefly on fish that occur near the surface, such as sand lance. Terns, by contrast, are plunge divers. Fishermen often use terns and gulls as indicators of the presence of fish. They say, "No birds, no fish."

A familiar sight as they hover over the wakes of boats or squabble over floating food, gulls are the true gluttons of the sea. They are characteristically social birds whose loud, querulous cries are as familiar echoing along waterfronts, estuaries, and beaches as they are miles out to sea. Long-winged, streamlined birds, gulls are not truly pelagic, but instead prefer coastlines and inshore waters for their itinerant lifestyle. Nonetheless, several species may be seen regularly attending fishing vessels on the Bank.

The great black-backed gull's prominent mantle—the back and upper surfaces of the wings—earns it such local names as coffin carrier and saddleback. A scavenger, this gull feeds on a dead sea bird. (VIREO)

Great Black-Backed Gull

Dwarfing virtually every other species of gull on Stellwagen Bank, the great black-backed gull (*Larus marinus*) usually attains a wingspan of more than five feet (1.52 meters). A sinister looking bird with a deliberate flight and menacing cries, the great black-backed gull is a ruthless predator. It preys on the eggs and young of terns and cormorants, as well as occasionally catching ducks and smaller water birds. It has even been known to rob members of its own family.

Herring Gull

The herring gull (*Larus argentatus*) is the most abundant gull in Massachusetts. Vast numbers congregate to scavenge dead fish or gurry from fishing boats. Conservative in neither its choice of food nor its habitat, the herring gull eats anything that comes its way, from carrion scavenged along the shoreline to practically any form of marine life, especially clams, crabs, and fish. The herring gull is as likely to find a reliable food source in a rubbish dump as it is on Stellwagen Bank. Abundant throughout the year in the Sanctuary, flocks of herring gulls are most visible as they squabble among themselves behind working fishing trawlers.

The mature herring gull has a gray mantle, a yellow beak with a noticeable red spot, flesh-colored legs, and black wingtips with contrasting white spots. (David Clapp)

Laughing Gull

A relatively small, distinctive species, the laughing gull (*Larus atricilla*) is characterized by its rather heavy, dark drooping bill and its black hood in summer. The species is named for its strident cries, which are reminiscent of raucous laughter. Like other gulls, the laughing gull has a distinctive feeding strategy for pursuing schooling fish. Approaching the school from the rear, the laughing gull

A flock of laughing gulls is a lively contrast against a backdrop of clear blue sky. (VIREO)

69

In full breeding plumage, the laughing gull has a pronounced black hood and broken white eye rings. (Bill Rossiter)

This immature black-legged kittiwake has a dark collar, a dark wing band, and a black bar on the tail. In contrast, adult birds have triangular black wingtips that look as though they've been dipped in ink, a yellow bill, and a deep gray mantle. (VIREO)

An adult common tern in flight displays its slender wings, deeply forked tail, and characteristic black-tipped, red bill. (VIREO)

dives for the fish near the surface. As the fish become aware of their pursuer, they swim farther below the surface. The gull follows the school until the fish resurface, and with renewed interest, resumes feeding.

Black-Legged Kittiwake

One of the few truly oceanic gulls, the black-legged kittiwake (*Rissa tridactyla*) is found offshore mainly in winter. The bounding flight and quicker wing action of kittiwakes distinguish them from other gray-backed gulls, even at a considerable distance. Often seen following fishing boats or whales to claim fish left behind in their wakes, kittiwakes also plunge-dive by hovering over the water and occasionally plummeting into the sea in pursuit of food. Among the most abundant gulls in the world, kittiwakes nest on arctic sea cliffs and in colonies in the Gulf of St. Lawrence. Their onomatopoeic name comes from their incessant *kitti-wa-ak, titti-wa-ak* calls.

Terns

From boats leaving Plymouth Harbor in summer, gyrating blizzards of terns are visible at their breeding colony among the dunes of Long Beach. Birds returning to this colony are often sighted with silvery sand lance and other small bait fish gripped in their bills. These fish are offerings to their mates in the early part of the breeding season, and later are food for their young.

Terns are also called "strikers" because of their precision dives while feeding on schooling fish. Spotting their prey with telescopic eyes, terns hover and then dive arrowlike into the water, often immersing their entire body.

Among the most elegant of the sea birds, terns have an exceedingly graceful flight that is accentuated by their delicately tapered wings and deeply forked tails. They also have extraordinary endurance and are noted for their long fall migrations to South America. These active and pugnacious birds are a familiar sight in harbors and on the Bank, especially during the late summer. Although eight species of terns occur as migrants or rare visitors along the Massachusetts coast, only common terns (*Sterna hirundo*) and roseate terns (*Sterna dougallii*)

A blizzard of common terns excitedly call to one another near their nesting sites. The least tern (with yellow bill) is the smallest of the terns in New England and an infrequent visitor to this coast. (Tessa Morgan)

are likely to be seen near Stellwagen Bank. The roseate tern is a federally listed endangered species whose largest North American colony lies in Buzzards Bay, Massachusetts.

Jaegers

Closely related to gulls and terns, jaegers get their name from the German word for hunter. Renowned for their piratical habits, jaegers feed mainly on fish, which they obtain either by harrying other sea birds or by dipping below the surface for direct catches. When the opportunity arises, they may also scavenge fish offal behind trawlers.

Their well-developed thieving habit is called kleptoparasitism. The jaegers relentlessly chase terns, kittiwakes, and other smaller gulls in order to steal their food. By swiftly pursuing their hapless victims, jaegers make their more timid relatives disgorge their food, which they in turn invariably seize in midair. This behavior has variously given them the names "sea hawk," "robber gull," and "teaser."

Pomarine jaegers (*Stercorarius pomarinus*) and parasitic jaegers (*Stercorarius parasiticus*) both have light and dark color phases. Parasitic jaegers are usually the more

Deep-chested and broad-winged, the pomarine jaeger is a powerful looking bird. In breeding plumage, this light phase bird shows a dark crown and whitish underparts crossed with a black breast band. The elongated and twisted central tail feathers are a distinctive feature of the species. (David Clapp)

common species. They generally arrive in greatest numbers in years when mackerel and bluefish are especially plentiful during August and September.

Phalaropes

Phalaropes are actually related to sandpipers, and they represent the smallest sea birds to be found on Stellwagen Bank. Like many shorebirds, phalaropes breed on the arctic tundra but are decidedly pelagic during the nonbreeding season. During migration and in winter, phalaropes feed and rest on the open sea in floating rafts comprising hundreds of thousands of individuals. Red-necked phalaropes, or northern phalaropes, (*Phalaropus lobatus*) are the most common phalarope species in the Sanctuary.

The phalaropes have earned the nickname "whale-birds" due to their preference for the same tiny copepods that make up the diet of the North Atlantic right whale,

Red-necked phalaropes are surface feeders, foraging where local surface disturbances concentrate zooplankton. (VIREO)

and to their odd behavior of picking bits of food or scraps of skin off the backs of whales. The most characteristic feeding behavior of phalaropes involves stirring up planktonic organisms by spinning in circles in the water, thereby creating miniature whirlpools. This peculiar habit apparently disturbs the quiescent marine life so that whirling phalaropes are able to capture it by quickly dabbing with their needle-thin bills.

Alcids

When the sea birds known as alcids take to the sea, they leave their awkwardness on shore. In flight, they generally travel in compact groups and keep close to the surface. To become airborne, they skitter across the water, rapidly flapping their stubby wings to gain lift.

The thick-billed murre is unusual in that it can dive to depths of as much as 250 feet (76 meters) and stay underwater for up to two minutes. (Blair Nikula)

Alcids are characterized by squat penguinlike bodies, small flipperlike wings, and striking black-and-white plumage. They establish immense nesting citadels on northern sea cliffs that enable them to breed in relative safety. Overcrowding is the rule in these colonies, with birds settling often for a mere toehold on the exposed sea cliff breeding sites. Collectively, alcid breeding colonies in the higher latitudes of the North Atlantic form the Northern Hemisphere's largest assemblage of sea birds.

As winter winds prevail and seas freeze over, these hardy sea birds head for the rough lap of the open ocean. During the nonbreeding season, far from any shore, alcids plumb the North Atlantic with an agility and speed that strikes fear into any herring's heart! They are pursuit divers that use their flipperlike wings to fly underwater. They feed on a diet of small fish and large zooplankton, in particular mysid shrimp and amphipods.

Six alcid species occur in the Sanctuary in winter. Five species occur rarely—the dovekie (*Alle alle*), the black guillemot (*Cepphus gyrlle*), the common murre (*Uria aalge*), the thick-billed murre (*Uria lomvia*), and the Atlantic puffin (*Fratercula arctica*). The sixth, the razorbill (*Alca torda*) is the most numerous in the Sanctuary. At the end of their two-month breeding season, razorbills begin a nomadic ocean life, moving to southern New England waters in November and December.

Right: *Looking like a caricature of a sea parrot, the Atlantic puffin sports a jumbo tricolored bill and seemingly spectacled eye. Although to us their appearance may seem comic, puffins are deft predators.* (Bob Bowman)

Below: *Razorbills are readily distinguished from other alcids by their thick bills marked with a white bar and narrow white line running to the eye.* (Bob Bowman)

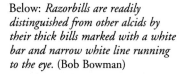

Razorbills are the closest living relative of the extinct great auk. They are similar in appearance to murres but have a thin, laterally compressed bill with a white line across it. The biting edge of their razor-sharp bill is a precision instrument that can capture and carry several sand lance at a time. Before diving, razorbills often dip their heads underwater several times in order to spot their prey. Like other alcid species, razorbills use their short wings with great efficiency in underwater flight, regularly propelling themselves to depths of 30 feet (9 meters) or more.

Loons

Loons are occasional visitors to Stellwagen Bank in late autumn. Common loons (*Gavia immer*), and red-throated loons (*Gavia stellata*) are the two species most often sighted. Common loons are birds of considerable size (32 inches or 81 cm long) and are famous for their distinctive and mournful tremolo calls, which awaken even the dullest ear. Praised for their swiftness in swimming and diving, loons have the ability to disappear below the surface with scarcely a ripple. Underwater, they can reduce their buoyancy by compressing their downy feathers close to their bodies, thus allowing them to swim to depths approaching 230 feet (70 meters). These heavy-bodied birds take off with difficulty, but once they are airborne their flight is swift and direct.

Although ungainly and awkward on land, the common loon, pictured here in winter plumage, is an unexcelled diver. (Peter Trull)

Sea Ducks

As the sun retreats and leaves the Arctic Ocean in darkness and cold, sea ducks follow familiar migratory routes southward, usually reaching Stellwagen Bank by October. Common eiders (*Somateria mollissima*), black scoters (*Melanitta nigra*), surf scoters (*Melanitta perspicillata*), and oldsquaws (*Clangula hyemalis*) all make appearances on the Bank occasionally.

Sea ducks are chunky and have broad flattened bills and muscular gizzards capable of grinding up the shells of mollusks and crabs and the bones of fish. Their heavy-bodied frames are well suited to resist the tremendous water pressure encountered while diving to great depths in pursuit of food. Once underwater, they use their feet and partially opened wings to swim.

Left: *Common eiders line their nests with their soft breast feathers. In Iceland, common eiders are protected and the prized down is collected from the nests without harming the birds. Pictured here in late autumn, the darker hen (left) and stoutly built drake bob peacefully on the water.* (VIREO)

Right: *The oldsquaw is the most loquacious of ducks. The male's yodel-like call is often heard before the bird is sighted. The male has strikingly long needlelike tail feathers.* (VIREO)

Filling the Bill

Sea birds have evolved different feeding strategies to meet the challenge of foraging at sea. During the breeding season, birds must find enough food to sustain the production of eggs and maintain growing chicks. During migration, adequate food supplies must be located to keep them fit for the remainder of the year. It's a busy schedule!

With the exception of specialized deep divers, such as sea ducks, most sea birds feed only at, or relatively near, the sea's surface. Food is often located visually, though some nocturnal foragers, such as murres, find prey by touch, and most tubenoses, such as fulmars, shearwaters, and storm petrels, apparently locate prey by smell.

75

BEAKS, BEAKS, BEAKS!

GANNETT

RED-NECKED
PHALAROPE

COMMON
TERN

ATLANTIC
PUFFIN

RAZORBILL

NORTHERN
FULMAR

JAEGER

HERRING GULL

Birds' beaks vary enormously in shape and size according to the species' feeding habits. Both the gannet's sturdy pointed bill and the tern's narrow spearlike bill allow them to capture and hold slippery fish. The red-necked phalarope's needle-thin bill is ideally suited for capturing small organisms. Puffins have spines on their tongues and the roofs of their mouths, as well as a notched bill, to help them catch and hold as many as twenty slippery fish at once. The serrated bill of the razorbill is sharp, an ideal tool to catch quick schooling fish. The fulmar and jaeger's hooked bills allow them to snatch surface-dwelling fish easily, while the herring gull's all-purpose bill is capable of handling a variety of prey. (Sarah Landry)

Sea birds are categorized as either good underwater swimmers or adept aerial flyers. Wings may be specialized for both flight and swimming, although to some extent they are mutually exclusive—the long or broad wings necessary for economical flight hinder underwater swimming, while short, narrow wings can best be used as flippers. The legs of sea birds are rarely adapted for walking on land; instead, their feet are often modified propellers or steering organs, expertly structured for underwater excursions.

Observing the feeding habits of sea birds can be helpful when trying to identify species. Noting whether birds plunge headfirst from a considerable height or dive from the surface of the water can immediately narrow the field. Variations in sea birds' anatomies allow them to pursue their preferred prey efficiently. Since most sea birds are specialized in their feeding behavior, there is usually little overlap in the size or composition of prey species or in the manner of prey pursuit.

Sea Bird Distribution

Wayne Petersen, Massachusetts Audubon Society

To the landlubber, the ocean appears flat, gray, and wet —seemingly devoid of contour or the differences in elevation and vegetation that characteristically influence the distribution of land creatures. While it is true that the ocean features that determine where sea birds will occur are different from those affecting the distribution of land birds, the influence of these features is no less profound.

76

Sea birds' feet come in all sizes, shapes, and colors—and they are perfectly designed for varying lifestyles. Most sea birds swim at the surface, paddling with webbed feet that act like modified propellers, enabling the bird to swim and steer with maximum efficiency. Deep-diving birds use their feet to swim underwater, often to great depths. (Tessa Morgan)

Both physical and biological factors determine the distribution and abundance of sea birds. In the first category belong such things as bottom contour, current patterns, water temperature, and water salinity. Of the biological elements, the distribution, seasonality, and relative abundance of plankton, marine invertebrates, and fish are most critical. Usually a combination of such factors explains why sea birds are found where they are.

On Stellwagen Bank, the factors that most strongly affect the presence and abundance of sea birds are nutrient upwelling (see page 38), or food availability, and water depth. Closely linked to nutrient production are natural fluctuations in the abundance of bait fish that serve as prey for many sea birds. In years when prey species are particularly abundant, sea birds gather in the relatively shallow and nutrient-rich waters of the Sanctuary in spectacular numbers to exploit the rich food resources.

Water temperature and salinity are the other factors that especially influence the distribution of sea birds on Stellwagen Bank. The best illustration of this is the differing distribution of four species of shearwaters—greater, Cory's, Manx, and Audubon's. The greater and Manx shearwaters are strongly associated with waters having cool surface temperatures and relatively low salinity, such as on Stellwagen Bank. The Cory's and the Audubon's shearwaters prefer waters with warm surface temperatures and relatively high salinity and are most prevalent in the warm, Gulf Stream–affected waters near the edge of the continental shelf south of Martha's Vineyard.

Besides these major influences, lesser events can temporarily concentrate sea birds in one area. For example, feeding whales and bluefish often attract foraging storm petrels, shearwaters, and gulls, as do the activities of working fishing vessels. A knowledge of these factors can

SPECIALIZED FEET

COMMON TERN

RED-NECKED PHALAROPE

NORTHERN FULMAR

ATLANTIC PUFFIN

RAZORBILL

POMARINE JAEGER

HERRING GULL

GANNET

Sea Bird Feeding Strategies

Piracy (parasitic jaeger pursuing kittiwake)
Some sea birds obtain food only indirectly from the sea. Stealing food from other birds (kleptoparasitism) is a way of life for jaegers, and occasionally some gulls, which initiate piratical attacks on their smaller relatives.

Surface Seizing (red-necked phalarope)
Many sea birds feed while sitting on the water or hovering near the surface, using their bills to seize large planktonic organisms, small fish, or fish offal. This strategy is commonly used by fulmars, storm petrels, phalaropes, and gulls.

Dipping (laughing gull)
Some sea birds pick up fish, cephalopods, or offal from the water's surface while in flight. This feeding method is common among gulls.

Plunge Diving (common tern)
Sea birds that lack the specialized features for underwater swimming can dive by plunging from the air, using momentum to overcome their buoyancy. They can reach depths of several meters by using this method. Gannets and terns, in particular, catch small schooling fish by plunge diving.

Pursuit Diving (black guillemot)
Many sea bird species are adapted for swimming underwater, often pursuing small fish and crustaceans to considerable depths. Most underwater-swimming birds use their wings as flippers (alcids), their feet (loons), or some combination of these two for propulsion (sea ducks).

(Sarah Landry)

PIRACY

SURFACE SEIZING

DIPPING

PLUNGE DIVING

PURSUIT DIVING

79

The gannet's frontally located pale blue eyes and its spear-shaped bill give the bird a somewhat formidable appearance. This bird was photographed at its nest on Bonaventure Island, Quebec. (David Clapp)

Below: *The Cory's shearwater has a wingspan of 44 inches (1.1 meter) and is the largest shearwater species in the North Atlantic.* (VIREO)

add considerably to one's appreciation of the events that determine where sea birds are found in the ocean.

How likely are you to spot sea birds during a trip to Stellwagen Bank? Sea bird numbers are highly variable from season to season and year to year. Consequently, the codes in the chart on the facing page provide only a rough indication of relative sea bird presence, not absolute abundance. Furthermore, the skill of an observer can seriously influence the probability of encountering sea birds on Stellwagen Bank.

KEY TO CHART ON PAGE 81

A = abundant   Species should be expected on 100 percent of visits.
C = common   Species should be expected on 50–99 percent of visits.
U = uncommon Species should be expected on 25–49 percent of visits.
O = occasional Species should be expected on 1–24 percent of visits.
R = rare   Species should not be expected on most visits.

WINTER: December–March   SPRING: April–May
SUMMER: June–August   FALL: September–November

Seasonal Status of Stellwagen Bank Sea Birds
(Wayne Petersen)

Species List	Winter	Spring	Summer	Fall
Common Loon (*Gavia immer*)	O	U		U
Northern Fulmar (*Fulmarus glacialis*)	U	O		U
Cory's Shearwater (*Calonectris diomedea*)			R	O
Greater Shearwater (*Puffinus gravis*)		O	U	U
Sooty Shearwater (*Puffinus griseus*)		C	C	U
Manx Shearwater (*Puffinus puffinus*)		O	U	U
Leach's Storm Petrel (*Oceanodroma leucorhea*)		O	R	O
Wilson's Storm Petrel (*Oceanites oceanicus*)		U	C	O
Northern Gannet (*Morus bassanus*)	C	C	O	C
Great Cormorant (*Phalacrocorax carbo*)	U	O		O
Double-crested Cormorant (*Phalacrocorax auritus*)		C	C	C
Common Eider (*Somateria mollissima*)	C	U		U
Oldsquaw (*Clangula hyemalis*)	U	O		O
Black Scoter (*Melanitta nigra*)				U
Surf Scoter (*Melanitta perspicillata*)				C
White-winged Scoter (*Melanitta fusca*)	O			C
Red-necked Phalarope (*Phalaropus lobatus*)		O	O	U
Red Phalarope (*Phalaropus fulicaria*)			O	O
Pomarine Jaeger (*Stercorarius pomarinus*)		R	O	U
Parasitic Jaeger (*Stercorarius parasiticus*)		O	O	U
Long-tailed Jaeger (*Stercorarius longicaudus*)				R
Laughing Gull (*Larus atricilla*)		O	U	U
Bonaparte's Gull (*Larus philadelphia*)				O
Ring-billed Gull (*Larus delawarensis*)	R	R	R	R
Herring Gull (*Larus argentatus*)	A	A	A	A
Iceland Gull (*Larus glaucoides*)	U			O
Lesser Black-backed Gull (*Larus fuscus*)	R	R		R
Glaucous Gull (*Larus hyperboreus*)	O	R		R
Great Black-backed Gull (*Larus marinus*)	A	A	A	A
Black-legged Kittiwake (*Rissa tridactyla*)	A	O		U
Sabine's Gull (*Xema sabini*)			R	R
Roseate Tern (*Sterna dougallii*)			O	O
Common Tern (*Sterna hirundo*)		U	C	C
Dovekie (*Alle alle*)	O			R
Common Murre (*Uria aalge*)	O			
Thick-billed Murre (*Uria lomvia*)	O			
Razorbill (*Alca torda*)	C	R		U
Black Guillemot (*Cepphus gyrlle*)	R			
Atlantic Puffin (*Fratercula arctica*)	O			R

FISH AND FISHERMEN

The sea is best handled by simple respect and
a wide berth.   —GLOUCESTER FISHERMAN

ISHING WAS ALREADY WELL ESTABLISHED on Stellwagen Bank when Captain Henry S. Stellwagen
first surveyed the area in 1854. "The Bank is known
by [the] vague term of 'Middle Bank' but little is ascer-
tained about it except that it is good fishing ground," he
wrote in his journal on October 27 of that year. By the
mid-nineteenth century, America's rapidly growing population had an appetite for salted and smoked fish. The
business of catching, processing, and transporting fish in
New England was centered in Gloucester, Boston, New
Bedford, and Provincetown, Massachusetts.

Because of their schooling habits and
former abundance, Atlantic herring
*(*Clupea harengus*) have long*
been the target of an important
commercial fishery in the Gulf of
Maine. (Nance Trueworthy)

82

Catches were bountiful in coastal waters. Until the Civil War, fishing occurred near shore with small open boats. In the 1820s, inshore catches of mackerel by hook and line increased dramatically. A Gloucester fisherman, for example, could land two thousand barrels of mackerel in one trip; a decade later, the catch was nearly seven thousand barrels. Beginning in the late 1840s, fishermen began using purse seines to encircle and capture huge schools of mackerel.

The fresh halibut fishery followed. Like the mackerel fishery, it exploited a species that previously had been considered unprofitable. These four-hundred-pound (182 kg) giants had been regarded as a nuisance by colonial fishermen and quickly tossed back. Between 1830 and 1850, halibut were plentiful in Massachusetts Bay. As inshore populations declined, however, fishermen ventured farther offshore to Newfoundland's Grand Banks.

As availability of certain species dwindled or fluctuated from year to year, new fisheries were created and old ones dropped off. Small dories and sailboats were replaced by fishing schooners, which could venture farther offshore and catch more per trip. At the turn of the twentieth century, diesel engines replaced coal-fired, steam-powered vessels and sailing craft. The early 1900s saw the introduction of otter trawls, which dominated local fisheries and greatly increased the capacity to capture fish. Inshore fisheries improved again with the introduction of mechanized gear and electronic navigational equipment. Primitive nets gave way to more efficient purse seines, gill nets, and otter trawls.

Historically, the term "fishery" embraces every method for pursuing and capturing aquatic animals, whether for profit or for sport. Within the Stellwagen Sanctuary, the term is applied to the capture of fish. Commercially important fish in the Stellwagen Bank region include groundfish such as cod and flounder, mid-water fish such as mackerel, and open-ocean fish such as bluefin tuna. Together they generate about $15 million annually.

Groundfish are dominated by the cod family (i.e., cod, haddock, hake, pollock), as well as flounders, dog-

*Northern shrimp (*Pandalus borealis*) are hermaphrodites, maturing first as males. After spawning as a male at about two and a half years of age, the shrimp undergoes a change, and by the following summer it spawns as a female. These pink shrimp grow to seven inches (18 cm) long.* (Tessa Morgan)

fish, and skate. Dragging is the predominant fishing method for groundfish in the area, but many fishermen use gill nets and longlines. Mid-water fisheries are highly seasonal, following the migratory patterns of schooling fish such as Atlantic mackerel, tuna, Atlantic herring, and bluefish. These species are caught using purse seines and hook and line.

Stellwagen's shellfish include crustaceans such as shrimp, crab, and lobsters, and mollusks such as scallops, sea clams, and squid. Northern shrimp are harvested exclusively in small-mesh trawl nets from December to May, and lobsters are caught in pots. Sea scallops, sea clams, and ocean quahogs are harvested with various types of dredges.

A fisherman loads fish boxes, called totes, full of northern shrimp onto a sling, ready for offloading. A full tote weighs about one hundred pounds. (Nance Trueworthy)

FISHING: DAY-IN, DAY-OUT

Do I love fishing? Well, yes and no. I've been fishing all my life. There's a lot of headaches to it. And you never know what the outcome is gonna be. I get up at four every morning. My wife says I'm out more than I'm in. Some days you make money; some days you don't. You gotta love it to do it.

—PLYMOUTH DRAGGERMAN

On a "mug-up" between tows, a fisherman, still in his oilskins, takes a break. (Neal Parent)

To the casual observer, the sea appears uniform. To the fisherman working Middle Bank and adjacent waters, the bottom is a series of dips, ridges, and troughs broken up by hard bottom (rock) and soft bottom (mud). Listening to a draggerman talk about Middle Bank, one hears details of this underwater world of sand and mud—unseen terrain detailed by cherished blips on a sonar screen.

An intimate knowledge of the finer features of the bottom terrain is indispensable for a fisherman —it spells success or failure. For example, fish will gather around a patch of gravel, a steep gradient, or an outcropping of rock the size of a Volkswagen. Conversely, an old anchor, a pile of loose boulders, or the rotting timbers of a shipwreck can ruin gear worth thousands of dollars.

A fisherman is a professional. Every movement and every decision is directed toward catching as many marketable fish as possible. He knows when to continue fishing and when to return to port. The well-worn nautical chart shows his familiarity with the spots he fishes. Not too long ago, navigation by dead reckoning meant combining knowledge of vessel speed, ocean currents, compass headings, and wind drift to estimate a position and chart a course. Just two decades ago, fishermen commonly navigated by lining up prominent landmarks. These estimates, however, depended on nuances—the tower on the second hill that looks like a camel's hump—and were sometimes restricted by poor visibility and other factors.

Today, fishermen use electronic navigation systems, including ship-to-shore radios, depth indicators and recorders, radar, "fish finders," and auto-

Studying his well-worn nautical chart, the captain is at home in the wheelhouse—the navigational center of the boat, housing the compass, radar, radio, depth sounder, and engine controls. (Nance Trueworthy)

matic steering devices. The state-of-the-art-equipment "ups the ante"—boats are expensive to buy and maintain.

Fishing is a tradition on Middle Bank. A Gloucester gill netter sips his coffee at an early morning bull session in the pilot house and wonders if his livelihood is at risk. On another day in early June, he steams out to the Bank, blanketed in thick fog, and hauls his gear, bringing up a thousand pounds (454 kg) of fish—it's a great day.

WHERE'S ERNIE'S HUMP?

Frank Mirarchi, Scituate fisherman

It seems to be a universally human trait to want to name things, and it comes as no surprise that fishermen have been assigning names to the features of the sea floor for generations. Fishermen use names as easy reference points for fishing areas. We tend to name places after the people who have discovered them (Pete's Tow, Ernie's Hump), or after their geographic location (Northeast Tow, the Half Hour), or after their physical features (the Mudhole, the Horseshoe). Rarely do these names appear on any chart, but anyone fishing the area knows the spots.

Fishing Is a Lifestyle

Many fishermen pursue a certain fishery for its economic rewards and for their own enjoyment. Fishermen are characterized as risk takers. To an experienced fisherman, the risks of fishing seem less than those encountered by taking public transportation, for example. The difference is in perspective; doing something with skill and familiarity does not seem risky. Fishermen are very conservative. A fisherman is no more likely to plunge into an unfamiliar fishery than to undertake a radical career change.

Fishing communities are often organized around one or more fisheries or gear types. For example, in Down East Maine the majority may fish for lobsters. In southern New England, fishing tends to be more diverse, perhaps due to the more seasonal availability of the different species.

The fishery for groundfish uses both mobile and fixed gear. Fixed gear, such as lobster pots and gill nets, stays put on the bottom. You set it, let it fish, and then come back to haul it. Since fixed gear stays at sea, it is sometimes vulnerable to theft and storm damage. When fish-

Frank Mirarchi,
Scituate fisherman

Jogging in a storm, the crew of a 150-foot dragger have already hauled the net and secured the doors. Working in fast-paced synchrony, they put down the last fish in preparation for the storm.
(Neal Parent)

A coastal lobsterman brings a load of pots out to the fishing grounds. (Nance Trueworthy)

ing is poor, fixed gear fishermen can choose to "let the gear soak" and do something else—maintenance, recreation, or an alternative job.

Mobile gear comes home with the fisherman every day. This gear includes trawls, purse seines, longlines, and dredges. Unlike fixed gear, which fishes whether its owner is present or not, mobile gear works only when it's deployed or towed through the water. A mobile gear fisherman's choices are to either fish or stay home.

In my home port of Scituate, Massachusetts, about seventy fishing boats share a small harbor with nearly two thousand pleasure boats. About fifty of these fishermen make their money from May through December from lobstering. Others supplement their lobster income during the winter by fishing for groundfish species such as cod and flounder. They use fixed gear, principally gill nets. The strategies, tactics, boats, and machinery are similar.

The remaining full-time fishermen of Scituate use mobile gear (bottom otter trawls). Most have never been lobstermen, and their dependence on groundfish is very high. Their boats are generally larger and less adaptable to other uses than those of their fixed gear brethren. The different fishing strategies and associated gear types therefore dictate the lifestyles of these two groups.

To our dismay, we are now increasingly facing times when fishing doesn't make economic sense. Reduced fish abundance and volatile price fluctuations can reduce gross income to where it barely covers the operating costs of fuel, bait, and ice. Continuing to fish under these circumstances is pointless. The number of boats idle at the dock during otherwise ideal weather gives testimony to this fact.

In contrast, the motivation to get the fish while they're here or while the market is hot is ever greater. Despite increasingly stringent Coast Guard safety regulations, the toll of lost vessels, injuries, and death continues to be unacceptably high.

A fisherman jokes that the other woman in his life is his boat. There is much truth to this. The demands of fishing require a commitment akin to raising a family. There are not only the hours on the water, but also the time spent on boat and gear maintenance, marketing, and, increasingly, strategic planning. Fishermen have long been viewed as long on work ethic but short on business skills. Out of necessity, this is changing.

Below left: *Docked at MacMillian Wharf in Provincetown, a fisherman's boat is another family member, often carrying the name of the captain's children. Provincetown is one of the few ports with a significant fleet of eastern-rigged draggers. On eastern riggers, the fo'c'sle, or crew's quarters, is forward (under the bow), the pilothouse is aft (to the rear, sitting on top of the engine room), and the net is set and hauled over the side.*
(Nance Trueworthy)

Below right: *On deck in his oilskins, a fisherman mends his net before setting out again.*
(Neal Parent)

Fishing is no longer a freewheeling succession of opportunities. Restrictive licensing, the capital investment required, and advance commitment to buyers are among the factors that can determine a fisherman's activity as much as the wind and the tide do.

Aside from these modern-day problems, a fisherman's work brings rewards no other occupation can match. Commonplace events affirm the conclusion that "My life is worthwhile!" A spectacular sunrise, the riot of sea birds wheeling skyward after a summer squall, the serenity of a harbor fog, and a thousand other scenes of beauty play endlessly throughout our lives. More than once I've looked up in frustration to find an indescribable panorama and realize that it doesn't get any better than this.

Personally, I find the greatest sense of fulfillment comes from a job well done. I can look at my boat, shiny bright with new paint, and feel proud. I feel a glow of satisfaction when I make a precise landfall after steaming half the night through trackless fog. Once, I donated fish to a chamber of commerce event and fed three hundred people. Words can never express how I felt, seeing those people enjoying my fish in a tent on a warm summer night.

But when I think of the future, my sense of satisfaction falters. I am certainly not the first person to live from the sea; I don't want to be one of the last. Maybe we've become too good at what we do.

It is not the fish for which I fear, it is the fishermen. The fish will not become extinct, only fewer. But that declining productivity spells torment for fishermen who must work ever harder to stay even. Soon we must learn to fish within our means—perhaps with smaller boats or more selective gear. If we cannot do this, my greatest satisfaction—passing the fishing tradition on to another generation—will be lost.

Dragging

Frank Mirarchi,
Scituate fisherman

Dragging is the no-nonsense practical approach to fish capture. Also known as trawling or otter trawling, dragging is the most common fishing method in New Eng-

THE PORTYGEE DAY OFF

Molly Benjamin

In the fishing towns of Provincetown, Chatham, and Sandwich, Friday is sometimes called "the Portygee Day Off," which means really only a half-day off.

Draggers and most other day boats don't fish on Fridays, mainly because the urban fish markets (such as New York's Fulton Fish Market) are closed on Saturday. So, instead of heading out, fishermen spend most of the day at the pier. Nets are mended. Winches are greased. Machinery is fixed. The list of things that need doing on a boat is never ending.

Everyone usually shows up to start the gear work in the late morning—that's about 7 a.m. Unless there's a particularly heavy amount of fixing that needs doing that week, they should be done about noon. A half-day off. With any luck, the fishermen will get a few hours of free time. A working vacation —that's a Portygee Day Off.

---

land. Draggers range from skiffs with hand-hauled gear to 150-foot (46-meter) stern trawlers that fish offshore year round.

There are day boats and trip boats. Day boats leave port before dawn and return to their home port in late afternoon. Their catches are prized as the freshest quality available. Trucks await their arrival and carry their catch to retail markets and restaurants overnight.

Trip boats are generally larger and have accommodations for crews of three to seven. Crews work in shifts, or

Fishing at sunset, a 75-foot (23-meter) western-rigged dragger is just setting out. The boat will make several tows through the night. The wheelhouse is in the front of the boat on western riggers, and the net is set and hauled over the stern.
(Alan Hudson)

91

"watches," around the clock, with trips lasting from three to ten days. The limiting factor is the shelf life of the fish. Most draggers ice their fish to preserve the catch.

Most New England draggers target mixed groundfish species: cod, haddock, pollock, yellowtail flounder, and winter (blackback) flounder. Formerly underutilized species, or by-catch, such as monkfish, ocean pout, and skate are becoming increasingly important. Seasonally, some boats also target squid, mackerel, butterfish, and herring—species not caught in conjunction with groundfish.

Modern dragging evolved from variations of the European beam trawl. A beam trawl consisted of a bottom net attached to a heavy timber that was towed by a sailboat. Some of the earliest fishery regulations (from the seventeenth century) restricted use of beam trawls at the request of hand-gear fishermen who could not compete.

Left: *Fish are dumped down the hatch into the hold below. Standing out of the line of fire, this fisherman is forking haddock into pens, which will be iced and packed until the pen is full.* (Neal Parent)

Right: *Buckets of cod are winched onto the dock, where they are weighed and boxed for transport to a processing plant.*
(Nance Trueworthy)

By the turn of the twentieth century, commercial fishing changed with the introduction of the steam engine and mechanized otter trawl gear. The first application of steam to fishing was in the use of a powered winch that facilitated the hand-lining of heavy gear. By 1900, all but the smallest vessels had a "donkey engine."

Otter trawl technology in the United States coincided with the advent of fresh, iced fish as a widely popular product. As the demand for fish grew, Boston became the primary fishing port for New England. In 1906, a group of Boston businessmen built *Spray*, a 120-foot (36.5-meter) otter trawler. Their investment proved profitable, and within seven years five similar vessels (the *Foam, Ripple, Crest, Surf,* and *Swell*) were built at a cost of fifty thousand dollars each.

Concealed Beneath the Waves: The Impacts of Mobile Fishing Gear

What are the impacts of mobile fishing gear on bottom habitats? This question has been of concern since the late 1300s in England, when beam trawls were first used to harvest fish. Bottom habitats are difficult to study because direct underwater observations are limited and costly. Today, research submersibles and underwater robots (called remotely operated vehicles, or ROVs) facilitate scientific studies of bottom habitats.

Recent research shows that trawl and dredge activities can dislodge large numbers of organisms that attach themselves to cobbles and rocks. Some of these undersea dwellers, such as hydroids, normally live only a year or less, but others, such as sponges, may be long-lived and not easily replaced once they are torn from their holdfasts. When these animals are brought up in nets, most are thrown overboard because they are of no economic value. While these organisms are not themselves target species for fishermen, they provide cover for fish and crustaceans—particularly juveniles—that are commercially valuable.

Peter Auster, NOAA Underwater Research Center, University of Connecticut

Richard Malatesta, SEA Education Association

Harvesting fishes and crabs that live on sand or mud bottom can alter habitat complexity. For example, rock crab, skate, and red hake make pits or depressions in the seabed, possibly to conceal themselves or to capture prey. Repeated dragging over the seabed reduces the densities of such species and may therefore alter these relatively "simple" habitats.

How much can a habitat be altered and still support a viable animal population? If we stop fishing in some areas, will fish abundance increase as habitat complexity increases? How do we monitor all these variables? Finding answers to these questions will enable us to better manage our living marine resources.

Longlining

Molly Benjamin

Surprisingly large numbers of fish are still commercially caught with hooks on Stellwagen Bank, particularly during the winter.

Hook fishermen fish for codfish using a style called "longlining." Somewhat like lobstering, it's a traditional kind of fishing that has changed little since the last century, when Winslow Homer painted men in dories hauling aboard longline-caught fish. Longlining is a style of fishing practiced by the area's more rural ports, rather than the big-city ports of New Bedford and Gloucester. Several day boats head for the codfish grounds from Provincetown, Chatham, Harwich, and Plymouth.

Longlining is often conducted from relatively small boats. Arriving on the grounds, the fisherman sets an anchor line with a buoy attached—often a buoy on a pole, called a "high-flyer," for added visibility. The anchor line is clipped to the longline, or backline, which is arranged in a box or barrel, with each baited hook sequentially looped over the container's edge. The quarter-mile line spreads out hundreds of hooks, usually hand-baited with chunks of sea clams and sometimes pieces of squid. This longline is anchored and buoyed at both ends.

The manner in which this line is set is almost breathtaking. Each longliner has a sheet-metal chute built onto the stern. As the boat moves ahead, the line actually flies out of the box and through the chute, hooks flashing.

SUPERSTITIONS—NEVER SAY PIG

Fishermen once used superstition to explain the inexplicable phenomena that permeated their lives. Even today, when fishermen understand the scientific explanations for many of the peculiar events they witness, superstitions are still regarded by many as ceremonial rituals. Many fishermen will eat certain food, wear special clothing, or perform rituals that despite having no logical basis still provide a level of comfort and, they feel, enhance the odds of a successful voyage.

Here are some of the strongest taboos. Never say "pig," never coil a rope counterclockwise, and never carry clothing in a black suitcase. Beware if you sail on a Friday. At all costs, avoid turning the stern of the boat "against the sun" when leaving the harbor. It's a bad omen if you see blackbirds before sailing. Whistling on the boat is taboo and so is sticking a knife in the mast. An observant fisherman will make sure the hatch cover is never flipped over. Lastly, a streak of bad luck will follow you if you kill a lumpfish!

Frank Mirarchi,
Scituate fisherman

*Not only are lumpfish (*Cyclopterus lumpus*) shrouded in superstition, but they have odd body parts. The lumpfish's fleshy pelvic fins are modified to form a suction disc that allows it to cling to rocks and other objects.* (Wes Pratt)

COD

POLLOCK

SKATE

YELLOWTAIL FLOUNDER

WINTER FLOUNDER

GOOSEFISH

SCULPIN

DOGFISH

HOW AN OTTER TRAWL WORKS

The otter trawl is a device for catching bottom-dwelling fish. The trawl net is constructed of nylon or polyethylene twine and works like a huge funnel as it's towed. The net tapers at the base to the cod end, where fish accumulate. The net may be towed over the seabed or at any mid-water depth according to the species sought.

The sides of the net extend in front to form "wings" to guide fish into the mouth of the net. The top wings are mounted to a stout rope called the headline. The lower wings and belly are attached to the ground rope, which is actually sections of heavy chain shackled together. The ground rope holds the bottom of the net mouth in contact with the ground and provides some protection against snagging. It also holds fishing lines clear of the seabed.

Floats and weights are used to keep the mouth of the net open. Spherical floats, made of material that withstands pressure at maximum fishing depth, are attached to the headline along the top of the net mouth to hold it up. Weight is distributed along the ground rope to hold the bottom edge down.

To spread the mouth so that it will cover the largest possible area, each wing is fastened to a steel

(Sarah Landry)

or wooden paravane, also known as an otter board or trawl door. Water resistance to the forward motion of the doors pushes them in opposite directions, thereby keeping the mouth of the net open.

The doors are attached to the net by steel cables known as bridles, legs, or ground cables. These are often covered with discs cut from old tires to prevent chafing as well as to enhance fish herding. A wire towing cable is fitted on the other end of the doors and attached to the trawling vessel.

There are variations in size of nets, net rigging, and gear adaptations according to the trawl fishery. One or two vessels may tow the net in mid-water trawling and bottom-pair trawling. Beam trawling deploys a conical net attached to a crossbeam that rides on ski-like sliders towed over the seabed. Although beam trawls are relatively simple to rig, their bulk makes them unwieldy. Recently there has been an upsurge of interest in using this method to harvest sea urchins.

Thousands of hooks are deployed into the water at a high rate of speed, with nary a tangle or snarl. Clearly, each box of baited hooks has been carefully packed to allow this to happen.

From roughly November to late May, cod gather in the deep waters surrounding the Bank. Longliners tend to fish "codfish gardens"—small rocky, ledgelike sites where cod gather. Typically, it is primarily the longliners who fish this "hard bottom," which is difficult to work by other fishing methods.

Longlining is an ecologically gentle method of fishing because the gear can only be used a few hours a day. It's set on the slack tide—the short period between high and low tides when the water calms down. It's only during the slack tide that the fish can get to the baited hooks and be caught.

The bane of codfish longliners are the vast schools of dogfish, which sometimes ruin a set. Despite the dogfish, the people who go longlining love it and know they produce some of the freshest fish available in America. The whole waterfront community agrees that hook-caught fish (sometimes called Chatham cod) are the best. Hook-caught fish command the marketplace's best prices for their widely recognized quality.

Seeking shelter against a ledge covered with seaweed, the cod spends most of its time foraging for hermit crabs, sea squirts, brittle stars, and other bottom dwellers. (Herb Segars)

COD

A heavy-bodied fish, cod (*Gadus morhua*) was the first fish caught when explorer Bartholomew Gosnold ordered his crew to lower a peach basket into the waters near the Peninsula Gosnold, which was later named Cape Cod. New England waters were rich with cod back then. Today their dramatic drop in numbers has brought many new fishing rules.

Cod can weigh more than one hundred pounds (45 kg) each. Records show that a huge 211-pounder (96 kg) was caught on a longline off the Massachusetts coast in 1895. Today, fifty- and sixty-pounders (23 to 27 kg) are not common, but even in the good old days, hundred-pounders (45 kg) were an unusual catch.

Cod can range from the surface to a depth of 1500 feet (457 meters). Unless they're traveling, they usually lie within ten feet (3 meters) of the bottom. Nantucket Shoals is the most southern portion of their range. Stellwagen, traditionally a prime fishing ground, has produced codfish by the barrel.

Mollusks are the mainstay of the cod's diet, but cod are omnivorous. Over the years, fishermen have reported finding everything from false teeth to wedding rings in their stomachs. Cod eat so many sea clams that the shells are sometimes found neatly stacked up like ashtrays inside their stomachs. They dine on hermit crabs, moon snails, sea clams, lobsters, shrimp, brittle stars (of which they are often crammed full), sea urchins, and sea cucumbers. They also eat jellyfish, particularly the walnut-sized ctenophores. They'll feed on squid, as well as on various small fish such as herring, sand lance, mackerel, menhaden, and even their own young.

One of the cod's biggest predators is the dogfish. Every fisherman has observed hundreds of cod with stunted tails, often a sign of a dogfish or bluefish attack.

Cod have been so important to the Massachusetts economy that the cod has been designated the official state fish. A wooden codfish hangs proudly in the State House, a symbol of the fortunes that have been built in this state from abundant sea riches.

Molly Benjamin

Molly Benjamin

FROM TRASH TO TREASURE

The wolf fish (*Anarhichhas lupus*) is knocking on America's door, and after decades of no interest, America is welcoming it. To human eyes, the wolf fish is one of the ugliest fish in the sea. Called a "catfish" by coastal New Englanders, this bizarre critter used to be routinely slipped back overboard by Cape Cod draggermen as they sorted out the catch on deck.

Like many species before it, the wolf fish is no longer classified as a "trash" fish by fishermen or marketers. Thanks in very large part to famous chef Julia Child, the wolf fish is now commonly available at fish markets everywhere, where knowing shoppers appreciate the lobsterlike qualities of this former reject.

The story of trash fish is a long succession of similar stories. English colonists used salmon and lobster—yes, lobster!—for fertilizer. The first labor contract ever written in New England conceded that the region's overworked indentured servants would not be forced to eat lobster more than three times a week.

The wolf fish is a solitary bottom dweller preferring hard ground. A weak swimmer, it spends most of its life nosing about among seaweed or rocks in search of a meal. When hauled out of the water, however, the wolf fish snaps like an angry bulldog. Its viselike molars can easily crush hard-shelled mollusks, crustaceans, and echinoderms. (Andrew Martinez)

Invariably, certain seafood is considered junk by one generation, and fishermen of the day have no choice but to toss most of it overboard. In time, however, species after species of fish find their fifteen minutes of fame and are ultimately treasured—and consumed.

Take mussels, for instance—the blue-black, shiny shellfish that as recently as the early 1980s were hardly eaten by anyone in America, although they were relished by Europeans. Mussels today are found in most white-tablecloth restaurants, ranked with the familiar steamed clams and other shellfish.

The same is true of squid, a mollusk that is seasonally quite common on Stellwagen Bank. For centuries, several million Chinese, Italians, and Spaniards had an appetite for the sweet taste of squid. Fishermen would collect some every spring, but just enough to satisfy European markets. Times have changed, and now squid is an everyday item on local menus.

A number of other Stellwagen species are moving to a status of heightened respectability. Fishermen used to avoid catching dogfish until recently, for Americans found them unacceptable at the dinner table. Since the 1980s, however, Provincetown fishermen have tapped a new market for them. Enormous quantities of dogfish, now sold at a good price, are routinely served in English fish-and-chips shops.

Even skates, the flat northern members of the ray and shark family, were regarded with disdain until a few years ago. Fishermen hated to catch them unless they were collecting a few to be used as bait by their lobstermen friends. The market has changed, and now numerous draggers work Stellwagen looking for skates. The primary market right now is in France and Belgium.

Bottom-Set Gill Netting

Scituate is a major port for gill netting on the south shore of Massachusetts, harboring a fleet of approximately fifteen boats that fish in the Sanctuary area. In winter, these boats are found mostly in the inshore areas of Massachusetts Bay. From fall through early spring, the fleet targets groundfish—cod, pollock, hake, etc.—on the eastern side of Stellwagen Bank. Generally, from March into June, they fish for flounder. In summer, the fleet moves beyond the Bank to deeper water. During the summer and fall, dogfish and monkfish are netted in the inshore areas of Massachusetts Bay.

A gill net is an upright panel of lightly constructed net made from monofilament fishing line. Its light construction makes it almost invisible to most fish. Fish swimming into the net can pass only partway through the mesh. When a fish struggles to escape, the twine slips in back of the gill cover, "gilling" the fish and preventing its escape. Gill net fishermen target demersal (bottom-dwelling) fish such as cod, pollock, or flounder. Mesh sizes vary from 5.5 to 10 inches (14 to 25.4 cm), to tar-

A bottom gill net stretches across the sea floor. Gill nets catch groundfish such as goosefish and dogfish. High flyers mark the end of the net on the surface. (Tessa Morgan)

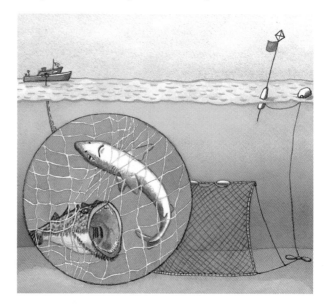

get fish of a specific size or species. Heavier twine is used for larger species such as monkfish and dogfish.

A bottom gill net is set on the bottom and anchored at both ends to the seabed. The lower edge is weighted with lead-cored rope while its upper edge is buoyed with small floats. Typically, a gill net extends eight to twelve feet (2.4 to 3.7 meters) up from the sea bottom. Each net is three hundred feet (91.4 meters) long. Up to ten nets may be joined, end-to-end, to make a string, ranging from 1500 to 2600 feet (457 to 793 meters). In common practice, one boat may fish thirty to seventy nets, divided among three to six strings. Flagged buoys on poles (high flyers) on the surface mark the upper edges of these net strings.

Gill nets are generally tended by boats in the thirty-five to fifty-five foot (10.7- to 16.8-meter) range that are fishing day trips. A Scituate fisherman describes the process: "We want to come home with a quality catch, so we usually set the gear one day and haul it the next, weather permitting. Fish are removed and the nets are immediately reset. Fishing is best on hard bottom [rocks or firm substrate]. Soft sand bottom is usually avoided to prevent competition with draggers."

A cod is "gilled," or caught in a gill net. (Wes Pratt)

A FISHERMAN'S PERSPECTIVE ON GILL NETTING AND PORPOISE PROTECTION

I've been gill netting since 1977. My first boat was a 36-foot (11-meter) Novi gill netter with eight nets, each 300 feet (91.5 meters) long. Today, my son, Scott, and I own the *Lady Irene*, a 44-foot (13.4-meter) gill netter operating out of Scituate harbor.

Bob MacKinnon, Scituate fisherman

Gill netting is a relatively small fishery when you consider the other types of gear fishing in the area. For boats 65 feet (19.8 meters) and under, it is an efficient way to catch fish. The nets are highly size- and relatively species-selective. The fishery is also fuel efficient; we set the nets, leave them to fish for twelve to twenty-four hours, and return to haul them.

Compared to other fisheries, there are many environmental advantages to gill netting. Most fish caught in a typical six-inch (15.24 cm) mesh gill net are four to five pounds (1.8 to 2.3 kg) and up; smaller fish swim through the large mesh. This allows fish to grow to a size where they have spawned at least once. Protecting juvenile fish is essential for sustaining fish stocks.

Gill netters' catches can also be managed easily. An increase in the size of the mesh by one inch (2.54 cm) or more, for example, allows more fish to escape and have a chance to spawn. Another management tool is to limit the number of nets a vessel is allowed to use. These simple, commonsense measures are easily put into place and enforced.

In the late 1980s, fishermen noticed an explosion in the herring population and a concurrent increase in the number of porpoises. At the same time, gill

"Catches vary from day to day, year to year." —Bob Mackinnon (Andrew Martinez)

netters began noticing a problem with porpoises getting entangled in the nets. Because gill netters are environmentally responsible fishermen, they joined representatives from the National Marine Fisheries Service (NMFS) and conservation groups to form the New England Harbor Porpoise Working Group. This group has proposed protective measures to NMFS and has generated research funds to develop gear that reduces harbor porpoise encounters with gill nets. For example, acoustical reflectors are being tested to determine their effectiveness in deterring porpoises from entering nets.

Gill netters are committed to resolving marine mammal interaction problems. We are family-based, family-owned, and family-operated fisheries. We want sound management of fish stocks, and we want to find the solution that allows fishing to continue while reducing harbor porpoise fatalities. Our livelihoods and the community depend on it.

Catching Dogfish—Intentionally or Not

Molly Benjamin

Sometimes the sound of barking dogs comes over the marine radio. Other times, listening to the fishermen's channel, you'll hear comments about "running a kennel" or a cowboylike tune about "Get along, little doggie." This colorful talk is how fishermen let other fishermen know that they have encountered a school of dogfish.

These small sharks can ruin the fishing for anyone seeking anything other than dogfish because cod and other groundfish will flee when the doggies show up. When a flounder or cod fisherman finds them in large-mesh gear, it can take hours of work to get them out and repair the damage they cause.

Bigelow and Schroeder, authors of *Fishes of the Gulf of Maine* (first published in 1953) wrote, "Voracious almost beyond belief, the dogfish entirely deserves its bad reputation. Not only does it harry and drive off mackerel, herring, and even fish as large as cod and haddock, but it destroys vast numbers of them. Again and again, fishermen have described packs of dogs dashing among schools of mackerel, and even attacking them within the

This deck load of dogfish will be gutted and processed for European markets. (Irene Seipt)

purse seines, biting through the net, and releasing such of the catch as escapes them."

But not all encounters with dogfish are unintentional, now that there is a market for them. The Provincetown fleet catches dogfish with a small-mesh net. Sometimes you will see a loaded dragger headed back toward Provincetown on such a slant you would swear it is going to tip over. The boat's list tells you that they're loaded up with dogfish and headed to the fish dealers. From Provincetown, capital of the underutilized-fish industry, thousands of pounds of dogfish are iced, packed, and trucked to a special fillet house in Maine. There the fillets are frozen in blocks, stored, and shipped by way of container ships to England, to appear in the famous "fish and chips."

Fishing Controversies and Regulations
Competing Interests

Frank Mirarchi, Scituate fisherman

Dragging brought the industrial revolution to fishing, and, inevitably, the change brought controversy. Belching clouds of smoke and spewing glowing cinders, these new trawlers moved with a clamor of machinery and hissing steam. They were greeted with trepidation by traditional fishermen. Steam trawlers caught more fish than dory fishermen, and this was resented. Moreover, the trawlers were owned by groups of investors, often fish processors, who were seen as a threat to the entrepreneurial tradition of fishing. Many small-boat fishermen

DOGFISH

Spiny dogfish (*Squalus acanthias*) average about
two to three feet (0.6 to 0.92 meter) in length.
Chiefly summer visitors to the Gulf of Maine, they
tend to school by size, and for large, mature individuals by sex.

Molly Benjamin

They travel in packs of thousands and can completely fill the screen on a fisherman's sonar fish-
finder. They are avid predators and are known to
eat herring and mackerel as well as other fish such
as haddock, cod, and sand lance.

A final interesting aspect of dogfish is their reproduction. Dogfish are ovoviviparous, meaning
they produce eggs that develop within the oviducts.
The female carries two to fifteen pups that grow
in her womb without a placental attachment. Each
pup is attached to a bright yellow yolk sac and
young are born free-swimming.

When a net full of dogfish is brought aboard
during the summer months, fishermen commonly
catch dozens of recently born pups. Even at such
a young age, there is no doubting they belong to
the shark family; each has slanted green eyes and a
definite shark shape.

*Spiny dogfish (*Squalus acanthias*) bear live young. A yellowish-
orange yolk sac attached to the developing dogfish embryo
supplies its nutritional needs until birth, some eighteen to twenty
months after fertilization.* (Tessa Morgan)

were appalled by the newer vessels. Some felt that the mere presence of such activity drove the fish away.

Conservation concerns quickly surfaced as well. Trawl nets could be unselective. As there was little or no science to nineteenth-century fishery management, most modifications in gear were dictated by market-based considerations that drove trawlers to catch as many fish as possible, as quickly as possible. Mesh sizes were smaller than those used today: 3-inch mesh versus 6-inch (7.62- vs. 15.24-cm), which meant that another contentious issue was the unknown effect of the gear on the seabed and bottom (benthic) species. Without the diving and video equipment of today, no direct observations of the sea floor could be made. Opinions on innovation versus tradition varied according to one's prejudice.

The Start of Regulation

Little was done to regulate fishing activity until the mid-twentieth century. Historically, national jurisdiction extended one marine league—about three miles (4.8 km)—from the coast. Three miles was the distance a shore-based cannon could fire with accuracy, so a league was a practical, enforceable jurisdictional limit at that time.

A winter (or blackback) flounder glides across the sea bed.
(Jon Witman)

The shape of a fish's tail fin provides a good indication of its speed and agility. Generally, fishes with squarish and rounded tails, such as the cod and flounder, are capable of sudden, short bursts but are comparatively slow swimmers. Fishes with crescent-shaped tails, such as tuna, are designed for high-speed swimming. The caudal fin of the dogfish has a much larger upper lobe than lower lobe. This design may give the shark, which lacks a swim bladder and must therefore keep moving to stay off the bottom, an added upward thrust while swimming.
(Sarah Landry)

COD

TUNA

DOGFISH

FLOUNDER

Most fisheries were confined to state waters, so the state was the primary regulator of coastal fisheries. During the 1930s, Massachusetts seasonally closed large sections of its waters to otter and beam trawling. Vestiges of these laws persist today: in the summers inshore waters are closed to draggers but open for lobstering.

The management vacuum in international waters (beyond the three-mile limit) persisted until after World War II, when the rapid development of high seas factory trawlers by foreign countries caused concern for offshore fishing grounds such as Georges Bank, Browns Bank, and the Grand Banks off Newfoundland.

The State Department and the military were not inclined to regulate foreign fishermen; they feared retaliatory measures by other nations against U.S. fishing and navigational rights. In 1976, Congress took action; they adopted the Magnuson Fishery and Conservation Act, or two-hundred-mile limit law, declaring that fish stocks within two hundred miles (320 km) of the U.S. coast were to be managed in the best interest of all American citizens.

With the Magnuson Act a national policy of domestic fisheries development began. This would be a revolution in U.S. fisheries more profound than that caused by the arrival of the *Spray* and its mechanized technology seventy years earlier.

Encouragement of an Americanized fishery took the form of federal incentives: low-interest loans and grants for vessel construction. Abundant capital provided the incentive to develop a host of new technologies for fisheries. Equipment beyond imagination in 1976 is available and affordable today: precision navigation instruments with twenty-foot (6-meter) accuracy in all weather, echo sounders that display fish on a video screen, hydraulic machinery, and high-strength plastics made into nets of unprecedented size and durability.

Today's Regulations

The Magnuson Act did more than eliminate foreign fishing activity off the U.S. Coast—it created modern fisheries management, which is still evolving to meet the needs of fish and fishermen. Fishermen now are required to obey rules far more stringent than the seasonal closures adopted during the 1930s.

Fisheries today are divided according to target species. Most groundfish must be caught with large-mesh nets (currently 5.5-inch, or 14-cm, mesh), which allow young fish to pass through. Squid, whiting, or shrimp fisheries have their own set of rules. Fishing is seasonally closed in offshore areas where haddock and yellowtail flounder spawn. Fishermen can only keep fish of specified minimum lengths, based on the species size at sexual maturity.

A school of pollock swim together, maneuvering in unison for mutual protection. (Sue and David Millhouser)

More restrictions are on the way. For years, headlines have announced the death of fishing. Some fisheries go down as others come in. The lifestyle and the people are resilient, but the resource may not be. To the fishermen, who live day to day, the future is worrisome.

What Controls Abundance of Marine Fish?

The vast majority of fish perish as eggs or larvae, either eaten by predators or exposed to unfavorable environmental conditions. For species like cod which produce large numbers of eggs (several million per mature female) probably less than one in 100,000 reaches its first year. Once a fish is big enough to swim vigorously—to pursue prey and to evade predators—its chances of survival improve substantially. After age two, fewer than one fish in five die from natural causes. However, few marketable groundfish like cod will survive long enough to die of natural causes; using state-of-the-art technology, humans can harvest over sixty percent of these young adult fish each year in our waters.

Estimating the effects of fishing on the long-term production potential of a fish population is a complex problem, because we do not yet have sufficient quantitative understanding of the natural physical and biological processes controlling population growth and reproduction. These questions are currently the subject of intense investigation and also debate with respect to the marine fisheries of the New England region.

The last several decades have seen profound changes in the composition of marine fish populations off New England. In 1976, the Northeast Fisheries Science Center (NEFSC) in Woods Hole, Massachusetts, recorded in the waters of Georges Bank an abundance ratio of three codlike fish (cod, haddock, pollock) for every dogfish and skate. By 1990, however, the ratio had been reversed—three dogfish and skates for every codlike fish. Fishery scientists have concluded that heavy selective fishing on the more marketable codlike species together with virtually no directed fishing (until very recently) on less valuable species is most likely the principal factor

The haddock's dark lateral line and sooty shoulder patch, called the "devil's mark," are telltale features that distinguish it from the cod. (Wes Pratt)

A fish's age can be determined by ringlike structures found in the small bones of the inner ear, called otoliths. The rings are more numerous and widely separated when food is abundant and growth is rapid (the light rings). In the cold months, growth slows down markedly (dark rings). By counting a white and dark ring pair as one year—from the inside out—we learn that the 22.6-inch (58-cm) pollock that yielded this otolith was five years old. (Frank Almeida)

triggering this shift. However, some scientists and many fishermen think that changes in the marine environment may also have been involved.

Nearly two decades of intensive study of the New England marine ecosystems by the NEFSC have not yet revealed any major changes in the environment *per se* that can explain these shifts in fish populations. It is unlikely that environmental changes alone would favor the population growth of dogfish and skates while at the same time depressing cod and haddock stocks, given the major differences in their reproductive modes and potentials. In any case, both dogfish and skates are known predators of juvenile cod and haddock, and skates are believed to be likely competitors with groundfish. There is now concern that these predator-prey interactions, combined with continued selective fishing, may compound the difficulties of rebuilding cod and haddock stocks in the New England fisheries.

The abundance of any species is limited by the carrying capacity of the environment. When a population is near this limit, individual organisms grow very slowly, just like stunted plants in a garden where proper thinning is not done. Also, when a population of animals is near the carrying capacity, its reproductive rate is necessarily very low in terms of the number of young surviving to maturity. When the population is significantly below carrying capacity, more food is available to the remaining population and growth rates of individuals increase. They also mature at an earlier age.

Such changes have been observed in both cod and haddock stocks off New England over the past two decades. For example, during the early 1970s Georges Bank cod reached 50 percent maturity at 2.8 years (i.e., half of the fish aged 2.8 years were mature for the first time), whereas by the early 1990s, the 50 percent maturity point was down to 1.8 years. Growth rates also increased markedly, with both cod and haddock showing significant increases in size at a given age. Scientists think that these species are probably biologically incapable of growing any faster, and that further increases in growth and maturation rates are unlikely. In addition, the heavy selective fishing on principal groundfish has caused major reductions in their spawning populations, which may have reduced the likelihood of successful reproduction under any given environmental conditions.

The jury is still out as to the relative importance of predator-prey interactions and spawning stock size in limiting production of cod and haddock; however, evidence is accumulating that the combined effects of fishing and predator-prey interactions with other species must both be taken into account when managing multi-species fisheries.

Sea Scalloping

American consumers have long had a love affair with scallops. The heart of the scallop industry is New Bedford, one of the nation's top-dollar ports because of the tremendous number of scallopers operating there. Numerous fish buyers in the region specialize in promoting the sale of scallops. Significant numbers of Cape Codders are also involved in the scallop fishery.

Scalloping is fairly straightforward. The boat pulls one or two rakes, or dredges, along the bottom. After a reasonable amount of time, they are hauled back aboard and the contents dumped on deck.

The rakes go back overboard to fish some more as the crew sorts the scallops and passes them on to the shucking tables. Sea scallops are shucked right at the fishing grounds, which explains why scalloping crews number between ten and fourteen people, typically far more than

Molly Benjamin

Scallopers come from New Bedford to fish Stellwagen Bank. Repairing the chain-link dredge is one of the many things to do on a fisherman's day off. (John Ryan)

Like clams and oysters, scallops feed by filtering microscopic plankton from the water. Along the edge of the mantle are more than a hundred blue eyes. Like the human eye, each has a lens, a retina, and an optic nerve that can sense changes in light intensity. (Herb Segars)

SEA SCALLOPS

Sea scallops (*Placopecten magellanicus*) make the ocean floor their home. The sea scallop is larger (maximum size about 6.7 inches or 17 cm) than the inshore bay scallop (*Aequipecten irradians*) which measures 3 inches (7.6 cm). The sea scallop's shell is generally about five inches (12.7 cm) across, with a reddish-brown top and white bottom. Sea scallops range from the Gulf of St. Lawrence to Florida and are most concentrated in New England waters.

To flee from attacks by predators, a sea scallop propels itself across the ocean floor by contracting its adductor muscle and expelling jets of water from its shell, sometimes making yard-long jumps.

on a dragger. Working at a special bench, crew members shuck their catch by inserting a scallop knife between the shells and scraping one side, then the other. The meat—the big muscle that opens and closes the shell—is flicked into a bucket. Later the scallops are washed with fresh seawater, packed in bags, and iced down in the hold. Having excellent shelf life, they remain there until the boat returns to port, where the catch is usually auctioned off to the highest bidder.

Shucking scallops is an art. Particularly skilled scallopers will keep a shell in the air continuously. One shell flies overboard, the scallop whips into the bucket, the second shell flips overboard, and another scallop is grabbed and shucked—all in a seamless process almost too quick for the eye to follow. Every year, a scallop-shucking contest is held between shuckers from New Bedford (and sometimes Gloucester) and Nova Scotia and the other Canadian maritime provinces. The shucking crown has gone back and forth for a number of years.

Harvesting Sea Clams

Molly Benjamin

Sea clams (*Spisula solidissima*) are called surf clams by scientists. They are found inshore in submerged sand bars, and are also common in deeper waters like Stellwagen Bank. An adult sea clam ranges from five to nine

*An underexploited resource, ocean quahogs (*Arctica islandica*) are often called "black clams"—derived from the Narragansett Indian word quahog, meaning "dark shell." They are collected by hydraulic dredge, then processed and sold to restaurants for making clam chowder. Congregating in sand or mud bottoms, these five-inch- (12.7 cm-) long bivalves can live for more than a century. (Tessa Morgan)*

inches (12.7 to 22.9 cm) wide. They grow rapidly, reaching harvestable size in about six or seven years.

Boats catch sea clams using big rakes that squirt water in front of the rake, remove the sand, and thus usher the clam inside the dredge. Usually they are delivered shoreside in the shell and trucked to houses where they are shucked.

Cape Codders walk out on the sand bars during the lowest full-moon tide of the year and collect sea clams for dishes such as sea clam pie and sea clam fritters. Sometimes they marinate the sweet adductor muscle, locally called the "eye." Marinated sea clam eyes are a much prized regional treat. Most sea clams are chopped and used in chowders or spaghetti sauces. Sea clams may also be cut into thin strips and deep-fried as strip clams. Longliners use sea clams as bait to catch codfish.

By extending its flexible, muscular foot into the sand, the surf clam digs in to conceal itself. (Andrew Martinez)

Lobstering

Lobsters be plenty in most places, very large ones, some being twenty pounds in weight. These are taken at low water amongst the rocks. They are very good fish, the small ones being the best; their plenty makes them little esteemed and seldom eaten. The Indians get many of them every day for to bait their hooks withal and to eat when they can get no bass.
—WILLIAM WOOD, 18TH CENTURY

Since William Wood's time, New England's regard for lobster has changed considerably. Today, the American lobster is New England's most famous edible ocean dweller, considered by many to be the king of seafood.

Lobstering provides a livelihood for thousands of Massachusetts lobstermen and their families. Since the early 1900s, the lobster-fishing industry has observed

Bill Adler, Massachusetts Lobstermen's Association

American Lobster, Homarus ameri-canus. *Lobsters have two dissimilar claws. The heavier "crusher" (right) is designed to crack hard objects like clams and mussels. The sharper one, the "seizer" (left), is used for catching and tearing apart prey into smaller pieces.* (Jon Witman)

minimum size limits—currently a legal lobster in Massachusetts must have a carapace length of more than 3.25 inches (8.26 cm) from the eye socket to the back edge, excluding the tail (abdomen). "Shorts," or undersize lobsters, and females carrying eggs must be returned unharmed to the sea.

Lobster traps are required to have escape vents large enough to allow any sub-legal lobster to leave the trap. Recently, Massachusetts lobstermen have agreed to limit the number of traps a fisherman may place in state waters—within three miles (4.8 km) of the coast. The "trap cap" in state waters is 800 traps; beyond that, there is no limit. Other conservation measures are continually being examined to ensure a healthy lobster population for the future.

Lobstermen believe that there may be two different populations of lobsters—an inshore and offshore population. Fishermen consider the inshore lobsters to be residents. Their movements may be limited to a few miles. The offshore population tends to prefer deep water. Offshore lobsters make extensive seasonal migrations in spring and summer, moving from the deep canyons on Georges Bank to the warmer inshore waters of Massa-

A rare genetic variation, blue pigmentation occurs in only one out of 30 million lobsters. Aquaculturists are especially intrigued by these specimens because they grow almost twice as fast as the normal greenish-brown lobsters. (Peter Auster)

chusetts. The move to warmer waters triggers molting of the hard outer shell, allowing the lobster to grow. In the fall, these offshore inhabitants return to deeper water.

Lobsters thrive in rocky and rubble bottom. The Stellwagen Bank Sanctuary is home to a population of resident lobsters that probably do not migrate, but since the Bank lies between the deep offshore lobster habitats and the inshore coastal locations, it may accommodate not only the local residents but also those passing through.

The American Lobster

The lobster's life cycle is fairly perilous. Female lobsters usually mate when their shell is soft, after molting. They can store the sperm in special receptacles for up to three years after mating. The fertilized eggs remain cemented under her tail for about six months. A female carrying eggs is said to be "in berry" because the eggs covering her abdomen resemble clusters of berries.

The number of eggs released ranges from ten to one hundred thousand, depending on the size of the lobster. Once the eggs hatch, the young larvae remain near the surface of the water for several weeks, molting as they grow. The vast majority of young lobsters never make it beyond the four-stage molt stage; they are eaten by fish and many other planktonic invertebrates. As typical of many sea organisms, out of the thousands of offspring a female may produce, perhaps one or two will survive to adulthood.

Above: *A lobster's eye stalks are extensions of its brain. Damage to an eye stalk stimulates a chemical reaction that causes the lobster to molt. Eyes cannot be regenerated, and if both eye stalks are lost, the lobster will die.*
(Kevin McCarthy)

Right: *A "berried" lobster is a female carrying eggs. The greenish-black eggs cemented to the underside of this female's tail are just about to hatch. When the eggs are first laid, they are black. Fishermen must return any berried lobsters they catch to the sea.*
(Herb Segars)

Those which do survive actively swim to the bottom to face another round of problems. Young lobsters prefer gravel bottom and dig tiny burrows and tunnels to hide from predators such as dogfish, skates, and codfish. Here their survival rate improves because the young lobsters have some protection.

In its first year, the young lobster molts about ten times and reaches a length of about one and a half inches (3.81 cm). Lobsters grow slowly. It will take from five to seven years for it to reach the size where it can be legally harvested. Lobsters have been known to grow to thirty to forty pounds (13.5 to 18 kg). These giants have been found in the offshore waters along the continental shelf.

Christy Karavanich,
Marine Biological Laboratory

SERIAL MONOGAMY

Lobsters are very aggressive animals and will rarely pass up an opportunity to fight other lobsters. Male lobsters have much at stake in these contests. The top male in an area will occupy a mating shelter and gets to mate with most of the local females.

Females close to molting individually approach the male and are allowed to enter his shelter. After cohabiting for a few days, the female sheds her hard shell and mates with the male. The male will protect the soft, vulnerable female for several days after mating. After her new shell begins to harden, she moves out and a new female soon takes her place. Scientists have termed this mating behavior "serial monogamy."

Sport fishing is a major commercial activity in the Sanctuary. Party boats carrying up to eighty passengers, as well as charter boats and private boats, spend long hours with hook and line. Tuna are jigged or trolled from June to early November; rod-and-reel enthusiasts fish for groundfish from April through October; and bluefish and scup (porgy) are caught from May through September.
(Barry Gibson)

Sport Fishing on the Bank

Sport fishing on Stellwagen Bank is a big business, with more than 200,000 charter boat trips annually. Commercial sport fishing vessels operate year-round, except during the harsh months of January and February. As with commercial fishing vessels, licensing and operation of sport fishing charter boats are regulated by state and federal authorities.

Before 1975, charter and party boats rarely fished beyond state waters (the three-mile limit), but with the decline of groundfish stocks, the industry has gradually extended further offshore, reaching the waters of Stellwagen Bank. Most charter boats are 35 feet (10.6 meters) or less, so weather conditions play a large role in determining whether they fish on any given day.

Saltwater anglers fish for a bouillabaisse of species. Early May, when mackerel are usually on the Bank, is the time to fish for the striped bass and bluefin that feed on the mackerel. In June, striped bass and bluefish lure anglers to try their luck. By August and September, the serious bluefin fishermen cast their lot. Additionally, cod, pollock, winter flounder, and summer flounder are targeted. The bluefin's smaller cousin, the yellowfin tuna, is also taken by commercial sport fishermen from time to time.

On some ideal summer days, hot spots on the Bank may be buzzing with up to sixty sport fishing boats—appearing as a tiny mosquito fleet.

This thirty-pound cod was jigged on Stellwagen Bank in mid-June.
(Barry Gibson)

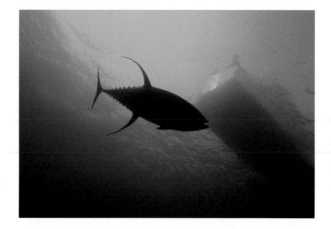

The yellowfin tuna's triangular finlets behind the long, scythelike ventral and rear dorsal fins are typical of this species. Yellowfin tuna are seen only occasionally in the Sanctuary. (Wes Pratt)

Fishing for Giants

Stellwagen Bank is a premier fishing spot for the highly prized bluefin tuna. The fish tend to be on Stellwagen from July to late October, sometimes into November. Bluefin lure fishermen who spend ten to twelve hours a day, for weeks, hoping to catch a fish. In August and September, the northwest and southeast corners of Stellwagen Bank can look like floating malls of "parked" tuna boats.

Tuna are caught with relatively primitive gear: rod and reel, handline, or harpoon. Regardless of gear type, tuna fishing is a costly enterprise, and there are no guarantees.

Over the last fifty years, the tuna fishery has changed dramatically. In the 1940s and 1950s, the commercial catch was primarily taken by handline and harpoon. In the early 1950s, fish landed in Provincetown weighed between thirty and two hundred pounds (13.5 and 91 kg). Fishermen had a tough time finding a market for the small tuna—under seventy pounds (32kg)—which they referred to as "footballs."

In the late 1950s, purse seining was introduced as a more efficient method of harvesting tuna. This method corrals massive schools of tuna that run near the surface into purse seine nets. Presently, the use of purse seining is controversial because of concerns over the status of bluefin tuna stocks and debate over the equitable use of the bluefin resource.

In the 1970s, Middle Bank became known among hand-gear fishermen for its giant bluefins. Fishermen on Stellwagen Bank and Jeffreys Ledge recorded bluefins weighing three hundred to fourteen hundred pounds (136 to 636 kg).

A few years later, the Japanese market for bluefin developed. Fish caught in 1972 were valued at five cents a pound; some of the fish caught in 1992 were valued at fifteen dollars a pound, one of the largest dollar-value fisheries in the Sanctuary.

For fishermen, the excitement of the hookup and fight is as rewarding as the dollar and cents value. The fish are generally "chummed" from anchored boats. Chumming means dropping chunks of bait off the side of the boat; the sinking food attracts tuna to a baited hook in the midst of the "chum slick." These giants require strong hooks, big game rods, and large reels filled to capacity, usually with 130-pound test line.

Once the expensive gear's in place, hours and hours can be spent waiting for fish to appear. Bluefin can show up as blips on the sonar screen, or the surface water may boil as bluefin crash through a school of bait fish. Being

In hot pursuit, a bluefin tuna chases a bluefish. (Paul Murray)

one of two hundred boats, you can only hope the tuna move in your direction.

Imagine the moment, after hours of waiting, after years of trying, when the fish strikes the hook! The excitement is heart-stopping. The drag screams—a hundred yards of line rips off the reel in seconds.

There are few comparisons to the sheer power of the initial run of a giant bluefin tuna. The crew rush around the cockpit to secure the angler in the fighting chair. The other lines are retrieved from the water. The boat is unhooked from the anchor, for the mighty tuna can tow a boat around the Bank. Muscle will strain on both ends of the line as the true battle begins, a battle that can last several hours. The outcome, no matter who is the victor, is sure to result in an unsurpassed admiration for the mighty bluefin.

The Titan of Tunas

Bluefin are striking in appearance. The upper body color varies from blue to black, with hues of bright metallic green. The underside is countershaded with gray and a mix of shiny white and silver, which can change rapidly to show bands of gray or more colorful hues.

Like squadrons of steely submarines, schools of bluefin tuna (*Thunnus thynnus*) cruise at speeds of up to fifty-five miles (88 km) per hour. These pelagic wanderers travel in large schools following ocean currents. Bluefin are sensitive to variations in temperature, food supply, and salinity, and are obedient to their ancient spawning instincts. Each year, bluefin make extensive migrations that drive them thousands of miles, from spawning grounds in the Gulf of Mexico to feeding grounds in the North Atlantic.

Bluefin usually appear on Jeffreys Ledge and Stellwagen Bank from July through October. Their presence seems to be determined in part by water temperature and by food supply. They occur in waters above sixty to sixty-two degrees F (15.5 to 16.6 degrees C) at the surface. Sanctuary waters also possess ideal oceanographic conditions for concentrating their prey: mackerel, bluefish, herring, and sand lance. The distribution, abundance, and age-class composition of bluefin tuna schools can

Show-stopping saffron yellow finlets and bright silvery cheeks enhance the deep blue pectoral fins that give the bluefin tuna its name. (Sarah Landry)

change drastically, however, from year to year, and also within a season.

Bluefin tuna are unrivaled predators. Their bodies are efficiently fashioned for speed. To reduce water resistance while pursuing prey, bluefin can pull their first dorsal fin back inside a groove. Their pelvic and pectoral fins can also fit into slots or grooves when necessary. The head and mouth are streamlined, and the body terminates in a large crescent-shaped caudal fin that provides tremendous thrust.

Aerial photographs show that bluefin schools are highly organized and segregated by size. This advanced form of schooling behavior results in cooperative hunting, which is unusual for fish. Their schooling behavior and physiology makes bluefin tuna some of the most efficient predators in the ocean.

Early accounts (1846) of bluefin tuna in Massachusetts refer to them as large "horse mackerel." Bluefin

How Tuna Keep Warm

Bluefin tuna are among the most advanced of fishes, one of the few that are warm-blooded. They maintain body temperatures warmer than the surrounding seawater.

Most fish normally lose heat through their gills. The bluefin has a special heat-exchange system that prevents loss of heat from the muscles to the gills and thereby conserves body (metabolic) heat.

Tuna have a large proportion of red muscle, muscle that is vital to their highly mobile nature. The dark red tissue has a high hemoglobin concentration, which allows it to carry more oxygen to support the tuna's high metabolism.

Maintaining a relatively uniform body temperature allows the bluefin to efficiently process large amounts of food and to grow at a high rate. The advantage of maintaining warm muscles is twofold: first, the muscles operate at a higher temperature, helping the fish to achieve higher speeds as an efficient predator; and second, the bluefin is able to extend its range to productive northern feeding grounds.

tuna are the giants among tunas and are one of the largest fish found in the Stellwagen Bank area. Weighing about two pounds (.9 kg) in their first year of life, they average about one hundred pounds (45 kg) by their fifth year, and may exceed 1200 pounds (545 kg) at twenty-five years of age.

A Fish Tale: The Voracious Bluefish

Molly Benjamin The big female bluefish watched a school of young mackerel swim by, then moved swiftly and efficiently, bringing death to many of the green-backed mackerel. Her head swinging back and forth, her mouth almost imperceptibly slashing from side to side, the big female attacked the mackerel from behind. Mackerel heads dropped from her chin to the crabs below, who were about to discover they were beneficiaries of a free lunch.

After a furious ten minutes, the water was bloody. A small slick had formed, and the oil calmed the water's surface. Nearby terns came instantly, recognizing the sign for what it was. Terns know that when *Pomatomus saltatrix*—better known as bluefish—go on a feeding binge, their prey often leaps free of the water in a desperate attempt to find an escape route. With bluefish behind and below them and sharp-billed terns above, the mackerel had no chance. Hundreds died this hour as dusk settled along the southern coast.

Supreme predators, bluefish often consume twice their own weight every day. Today, though, the group feeding forays have slowed. A school of sand lance swims unknowingly close, but go unmolested.

Part of an ever tightening school of bluefish, our female *Pomatomus* is swimming farther offshore as spawning season approaches. Ultimately they are headed for the edge of the Gulf Stream. Six years old now, this female bluefish has been spawning with her peers since the

A bluefish's snapping jaws sweep through a school of mackerel.
(Tessa Morgan)

age of two. Her first year, she spewed forth more than a million eggs. Now she is bigger, stronger, and will cast off twice that number, to be fertilized by sperm provided by the males in her group. Within days, the fertilized eggs will hatch, and the yolk sacs will be quickly consumed by the young larvae, who from their first days display the voracious appetites that have made their kind famous. The larvae will ride along near the surface, bobbing in the currents slowly, inexorably moving inshore.

Months later, this female is among the first wave of bluefish to surround the island of Martha's Vineyard. A fine fifteen-pound (6.8 kg) specimen, she will escape the rain of lures and flies the island fishermen throw her way, but eventually this super predator is devoured by an even stronger and larger hunter, a bluefin tuna.

The Fish Species of Stellwagen Bank

Among ancient Egyptians, the fish was sacred (their deity Isis had a fish head) and early Syrian and African tribes adopted the fish as a religious symbol. In astronomy and astrology, the twelfth sign of the Zodiac is Pisces, the Fishes.

The myth and mystery of fishes persist. The sea serpent probably has its origins in sightings of rarely seen fishes such as basking sharks, giant eels, snakelike oar fish, or even sunfishes. Over the last thousand years, rains of fishes (and frogs) have been witnessed many times in Europe and India. So far, no showers of mermaids, mermen, or sea serpents have fallen.

In everyday speech, the word "fish" is often used erroneously to include any animal living in the water, such as whales, shellfish, starfish, and jellyfish. All true fish are vertebrates (animals with backbones), whereas shellfish, starfish, and jellyfish are invertebrates. For the record, a true fish is loosely defined as an aquatic vertebrate that propels and balances itself with fins and obtains oxygen from the water by means of gills. Ichthyology, the branch of zoology that deals with the study of fishes, classifies them into two groups of jawless fishes (hagfish and lampreys) and two groups with jaws—cartilaginous fishes (sharks, skates, rays), and bony fishes (all the rest).

*Loafing along with its mouth agape, the basking shark (*Cetorrhinus maimus*) feeds by straining millions of minute crustaceans from the seawater with its comblike gill rakers. Dwarfing the divers above, this 30-foot (9-meter) basking shark appears undisturbed by their presence.* (Center for Marine Conservation)

*The sleek blue shark (*Prionace glauca*) is frequently seen at the surface, swimming lazily with its first dorsal fin and the tip of the tail out of the water.* (Paul Erickson)

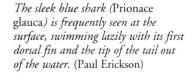

*The little skate (*Raja erinacea*) grows no larger than 20 inches (51 cm). The skate's habit of settling on the bottom and throwing sand over its back provides camouflage as it waits for its prey, which includes unsuspecting crabs, squid, clams, and worms.* (Sue and David Millhouser)

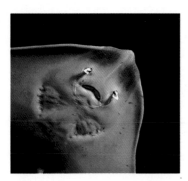

The underside of a skate's head has five small gill openings below the mouth. (Sue and David Millhouser)

Bony fishes (in the class Osteichthyes) include all the finfishes and are made up of more than twenty thousand species worldwide. Sharks and skates have skeletons made entirely of cartilage like the tough, flexible tissue found in the tip of your nose. Because they lack true bones, sharks and skates belong to a separate class of fishes called Chondrichthyes, which means cartilaginous fishes. This class also includes their relatives, the rays and chimeras.

Judging from the many and varied forms of fishes, body shapes are clearly not arbitrary. Their bodies conform efficiently to their particular mode of life. The mackerel, for example, is a pelagic, or open water, fish that depends on speed to obtain its food and escape from its enemies. Every line and rounded contour of its cigar-shaped body is suggestive of swift motion. Its bullet-shaped head and pointed snout aid its rapid movement. The flattened form of the skate gives a decided advantage to this groundfish by enabling it to burrow into the sand on the sea floor and escape detection by prey or predator.

Although their body forms vary, fish have a basic similarity in their swimming movements. Contrary to popular belief, most fish do not actually swim with their side or back fins. Generally, their fins serve as stabilizers, hydroplanes, rudders, or even brakes. Their main propellant is body movement, along with the side-to-side pushing action of the tail and the jet-action of water through the gills during breathing. Fins are certainly

All skates produce eggs enclosed in a black case with four long tendrils that anchor it to the bottom. The embryo takes the better part of a year to develop and finally emerges as a small edition of the adult. The empty egg cases, called mermaids' purses, are commonly found along beaches. (Tessa Morgan)

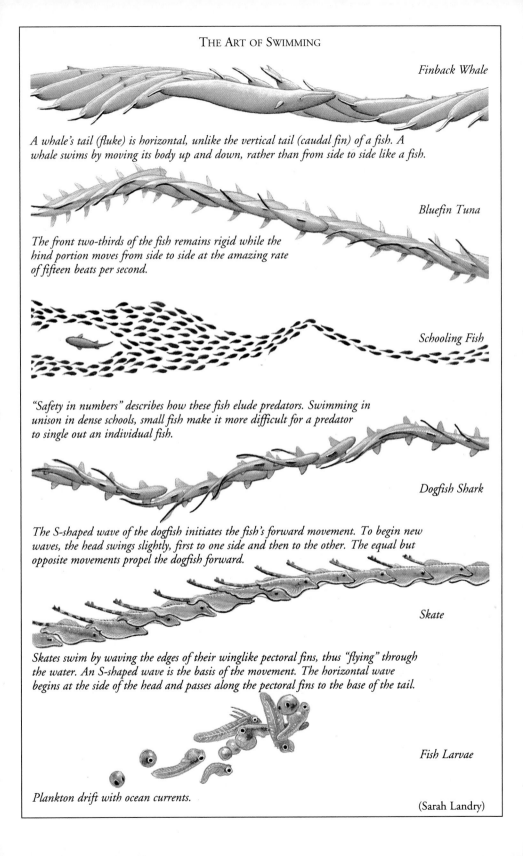

THE ART OF SWIMMING

Finback Whale

A whale's tail (fluke) is horizontal, unlike the vertical tail (caudal fin) of a fish. A whale swims by moving its body up and down, rather than from side to side like a fish.

Bluefin Tuna

The front two-thirds of the fish remains rigid while the hind portion moves from side to side at the amazing rate of fifteen beats per second.

Schooling Fish

"Safety in numbers" describes how these fish elude predators. Swimming in unison in dense schools, small fish make it more difficult for a predator to single out an individual fish.

Dogfish Shark

The S-shaped wave of the dogfish initiates the fish's forward movement. To begin new waves, the head swings slightly, first to one side and then to the other. The equal but opposite movements propel the dogfish forward.

Skate

Skates swim by waving the edges of their winglike pectoral fins, thus "flying" through the water. An S-shaped wave is the basis of the movement. The horizontal wave begins at the side of the head and passes along the pectoral fins to the base of the tail.

Fish Larvae

Plankton drift with ocean currents.

(Sarah Landry)

used for slow swimming, but if prey appear or danger threatens, body movements quickly come into play.

Pliny the Elder (circa A.D. 200) triumphantly cataloged 176 fish species. He exclaimed, "In the sea and the ocean, vast as it is, there exists, by Hercules! nothing that is unknown to us, and a truly marvelous feat it is that we are best acquainted with those things which Nature had concealed in the deep."

Today we know that he drastically underestimated the number of fish species in the world. The Stellwagen Bank Sanctuary harbors at least 135 species. Some species stay here year-round. Others depart when food becomes scarce, when water temperatures change, when spawning instincts dictate, or for reasons we have yet to understand.

The fish species in the Sanctuary fall into two groups: demersal, those living on or near the seabed, and pelagic, those living in open water. Demersal fish, more commonly called groundfish, include cod, haddock, pollock, hake, dogfish, goosefish, sculpins, skate, and cusk, as well as flatfish, including flounders. The movements of groundfish are affected both by seasonal changes in water temperature and by the type of substrate, or bottom. Some of these fish are found exclusively on the sea floor, feeding on benthic organisms, while others are found just above the bottom.

Left: *A member of the sculpin family, the sea raven (*Hemitripterus americanus*) has many distinctive characteristics—the ragged outline of its dorsal fin, the fleshy tabs on its lower jaw, and its large, fleshy pectoral fins, to name a few. Fanlike pectoral fins typify the sculpin family. Sculpins can vary their color according to their surroundings.* (Kevin McCarthy)

Right*: Acadian redfish (*Sebastes fasciatus*), now a popular table fish marketed as "ocean perch," was once used as lobster bait. Redfish are slow-growing, maturing at about six years of age, and may live for more than forty years. Females are ovoviviparous—their young hatch internally before being released into the sea.* (Jon Witman)

HOW DO FISH BREATHE?

Fish breathe with their gills. Water, continually taken in through the mouth, passes backward over the gills and escapes under the free back edge of the gill cover. The gills contain many finely divided blood vessels. As blood is pumped to the gills by the heart, it passes through these fine blood vessels, where it absorbs oxygen from the water and releases carbon dioxide. The freshly oxygenated blood then is pumped on to different parts of the body.

The more common pelagic fish in the Sanctuary include herring, mackerel, sharks, bluefish, bluefin tuna, sand lance, and menhaden. Most of these schooling fish are sensitive to temperature changes and move between inshore and offshore waters. Some, like the cod, migrate north to colder Maine waters each summer; others, like bluefish and bluefin tuna, head south in the fall as northeasterly winds blow and temperatures drop.

Massachusetts Bay acts like a catch basin for a number of these species due to its location at the southwestern end of the Gulf of Maine. Many fish such as cod, haddock, silver hake, witch flounder, and sea dabs spawn on Stellwagen Bank and nearby inshore waters. The currents carry eggs and larvae in an endless track around the Gulf of Maine, where young fish grow and mature, in nature's never ending cycle.

Goosefish

Goosefish (*Lophius americanus*) are some of the most peculiar fish in the sea. These flat bottom dwellers are all mouth, and their gape is something to see. Beneath their enormous head, they taper quite elegantly. They can grow to over four feet (1.2 meters) long and weigh more than 50 pounds (22.5 kg).

Molly Benjamin

On deck, fishermen are always on the lookout for goosefish because nobody wants to let a hand or a foot come near that enormous maw, not even if they are wearing rubber boots or gloves! Almost invariably, the goosefish on deck has fish in its mouth.

Camouflaged by its flattened, irregular shape, the goosefish is one of many sea creatures that lie in wait for their prey. The first spine of its dorsal fin is modified to form a "fishing pole" with an attached fleshy lure on the tip. When a victim approaches to investigate the lure, the goosefish abruptly opens its mouth. Water rushes into the gaping maw, taking with it the unfortunate prey. Goosefish have been known to swallow crabs, fish, and sea birds. (Sue and David Millhouser)

Goosefish have remarkable appetites. They have been found with thirty-inch (76 cm) halibut in their stomachs. Some have been found with seventy-five herring, as well as dogfish, cod, flounder, and skates, and another goosefish had seven ducks in one meal!

In addition to its massive mouth, the goosefish has another quite unusual appendage: a "fishing rod" mounted just above its jaws. Researchers report watching the goosefish dangle its "lure"—the flap of skin at the tip of its dorsal fin—and quickly engulf the first fish that investigates.

These heady creatures are found in shallow water as well as on the deepest slope of the continental shelf. They're found on every kind of bottom. Goosefish spawn anywhere and almost at any time except deepest winter.

Flatfish

Undulating through the water like flying carpets, flatfish glide to the bottom, flick sand onto their backs, and vanish except for protruding eyes and mouth. The flatfish are an unusual tribe, so different from all other fish that no one is likely to mistake them. Unlike other flat-bodied fish, such as the goosefish, described above, the true flatfish do not lie on their bellies but on their left or right side.

Most female flatfish may deposit more than a half million eggs that float in the upper surface layers for up

to two weeks before they hatch. As larvae, flatfish look like any other fish, with an eye on each side of the head and a horizontal mouth, but when the larval fish is about half an inch long, a metamorphosis occurs. As the larvae grow, the body begins to tilt to one side, the mouth twists, and one eye migrates to the other side of the head, either to the left or right side, depending on the species. All this shifting leaves one side of the fish "blind"—this becomes the underside. Flatfish are classified as right-eyed or left-eyed according to the side on which the eyes are located.

While these radical changes take place, the little fish sinks to the bottom. For the remainder of its life the adult flatfish lies on its blind side. The top side (where the eyes are located) is often colored brown with distinctive spots or blotches, so the fish can blend with its surroundings. Masters of disguise, flatfish are adept at changing the color of their pigmented side to match that of the seabed on which they live.

Left: *The floating egg veil of the goosefish may be up to thirty-five feet (10.7 meters) long and carry more than a million eggs.* (Wes Pratt)

Right: *Each goosefish egg has an oil globule (center) that helps keep the egg afloat.* (Wes Pratt)

The fleshy lips and closely set eyes of the winter flounder are typical of all flatfish. (Andrew Martinez)

YELLOWTAIL
FLOUNDER

WINTER
FLOUNDER

AMERICAN
PLAICE

WINDOWPANE
FLOUNDER

(Sarah Landry)

FLATFISH

Yellowtail Flounder (*Pleuronectes ferrugineus*)
The yellowtail flounder starts life as a tiny, translucent egg, smaller than one millimeter. The egg is buoyant and floats near the surface. Upon hatching, the larval fish may drift freely for more than a month, at the mercy of the prevailing current.

The young fish starts life with an eye on each side of its head and a horizontal mouth. As the larva grows, one eye migrates to the other side of the head and the mouth twists. The periods of larval growth and metamorphosis vary among species and are governed by water temperature. The process may take up to four months for fish in the Gulf of Maine. As the small flounder grows, it sinks to the bottom. It spends its adult life on the seabed, lying permanently on one side, left or right.

Winter Flounder (*Pleuronectes americanus*)
The winter, or blackback, flounder makes small seasonal migrations to estuaries and bays to spawn during the winter. In summer it moves into deeper water.

American Plaice (*Hippoglossoides platessoides*)
The American plaice, or dab, has a large mouth like the halibut. Characteristic of many flatfish, it avoids rocky or hard bottom, preferring a mixture of sand and mud.

Windowpane Flounder (*Scophthalmus aquosus*)
Known locally as sand dab, windowpane flounders are so named because of their extreme thinness. When held up to the light, a sand dab's body appears translucent. They are shoal-water fish; their upper limit is just below the tide mark and lower limit is probably around the 120- to 150-foot (36.6- to 45.7-meter) line.

Although adult flatfish are normally bottom dwellers, swimming with their eyeless side down, some species, such as the large halibut—which grows to over six and a half feet (2 meters)—actively swim in mid-water to catch prey. All flatfish are carnivorous. Depending on the species, they eat a variety of sea animals—sea worms, small amphipods and crabs, and other fish—relying on their sense of smell and visual acuity to locate prey.

Commercially important flatfish in the Sanctuary include both the right-eyed flounders: American plaice (dab), winter flounder (blackback or lemon sole), yellowtail flounder, and witch flounder (gray sole); and left-eyed flounders: four-spot flounder, summer flounder (fluke), and windowpane flounder (sand dab or brill).

Some species are residents in all seasons (windowpane, yellowtail, winter flounder), while others are common in warm months (four-spot flounder), typically moving farther offshore or southward when temperatures cool. Other species like the American plaice are common in cold months, moving north or east into deeper waters in the summer.

The Incredible Hulk: Ocean Sunfish

Whale watchers are often startled by a sharklike fin flopping from side-to-side on the surface. After catching their breath, the ocean wise realize they're looking at an ocean sunfish.

The giant ocean sunfish, or *Mola mola* (Latin for millstone) resembles a huge pancake. Its flattened body has two enlarged fins, one dorsal fin projecting upward like a sail, and an anal fin projecting down like a centerboard. The truncated tail, or clavus, covers the rear end of the body in a scalloped fold of skin. A protruding brow and small, beaklike mouth accentuate the sunfish's all-head appearance. The mola's tough skin, nearly six inches

An ocean sunfish begins life as one of millions of free-floating eggs. When the larva hatches, it is covered with horny knobs that soon change into thumbtacklike spines. It is only one-eighth of an inch (3 mm) long. On a juvenile, these spines look like fencing swords, jutting out in all directions.
(Sarah Landry)

thick in some individuals, armors the fish against most of its enemies.

The ocean sunfish is a solitary, pelagic fish. The gentle movements of the enormous dorsal and anal fins cause the fish to yaw in a passive, sluggish manner when near the surface. Moving slowly with its mouth open, it drifts about in a constant quest of nature's offerings, dining primarily on jellyfish, comb jellies, and other planktonic organisms. This strange creature often basks near the surface, a behavior that inspired its common name.

Despite its imposing hulk, as much as ten feet (3 meters) in length and more than a ton (907 kg) in weight, the ocean sunfish is harmless.
(Herb Segars)

VESSEL TRAFFIC IN SANCTUARY WATERS

Full fathom five thy father lies,
Of his bones are coral made;
Those are pearls that were his eyes:
Nothing of him that doth fade,
But doth suffer a sea change
Into something rich and strange.

WILLIAM SHAKESPEARE

Victor T. Mastone, Massachusetts
Board of Underwater
Archaeological Resources

STELLWAGEN BANK IS THE GATEWAY to Massachusetts' maritime commerce. Ever since Europeans settled in New England, major shipping lanes have crossed Stellwagen Bank. Today, oil tankers, colliers, container barges, trawlers, and pleasure boats have replaced coastal schooners, clipper ship, packets, and fishing schooners.

Until the opening of the Cape Cod Canal, the only way to approach the ports inside Massachusetts Bay—Boston, Plymouth, Salem, Gloucester, and Provincetown—was around Cape Cod and across Stellwagen Bank. Once the canal was opened in 1914, vessel traffic increased, and the late nineteenth and early twentieth centuries saw the highest level of coastal shipping in the Northeast.

Shipwrecks

Natural hazards and human error have combined to cause a significant number of shipwrecks in, or adjacent to, the Stellwagen Bank area. Not surprisingly, shipwrecks are most frequent during major storms. By contrast, when weather is not the culprit, collisions and founderings are the major cause of vessel loss. Further, a strong seasonal distribution of shipwrecks, with the peak period of November and December, is exhibited off the Massachusetts coast. The harsh weather of the winter months results in higher numbers of shipwrecks even though total traffic volume is typically lowest at that time of year.

Adverse and unpredictable weather conditions, such as severe gales and hurricanes, have been identified as the major cause of vessel loss. There were as many as twenty major storms in the Massachusetts Bay area between 1676 and 1898. The Triple Hurricanes of December 1839 and the Portland Gale of November 1898 were particularly devastating.

The 1839 storms inspired Longfellow's poem "The Wreck of the *Hesperus.* " Contemporary accounts noted over two hundred vessels sunk in Boston Harbor alone, with comparable losses in the ports of Gloucester and Provincetown.

By comparison, roughly four hundred vessels were lost during the Portland Gale (1898). The greatest number of shipwrecks to occur in one year for New England happened during that year, with 90 percent of those shipwrecks taking place in just three days, November 25 to 27. During this devastating storm, the steamship *Portland,* and all of its 160 passengers and crew members on board were lost. The storm was named "The Portland Gale of 1898" after this most famous of all New England shipwrecks.

The *Portland,* a 291-foot (88.7-meter) side-wheeled paddle-steamer, was built in 1890 by the New England

The S.S. Portland went down with 160 passengers in the Portland Gale of 1898. Recently, remains of the wreck have been found close to the northern boundary of the Sanctuary. (The Maine Historical Society)

The gateway to the maritime commerce of Massachusetts, the shipping lanes that pass through Stellwagen Bank accommodate more than 2500 vessels a year.
(Brian Walski, Boston Herald)

Shipbuilding Company of Bath, Maine. It had a gross weight of 2283 tons and its top speed was fifteen knots. It served the Portland Steam Packet Company in its Boston to Portland line.

The loss of the *Portland* was shrouded in mystery for almost a century. Only a small number of bodies were ever recovered. Debris began washing up on the shores of Cape Cod shortly after the wreck, but the remains of the side-wheeler were not found until just a few years ago—not near Cape Cod, but farther north, off the coast of Gloucester, near Stellwagen Bank.

The *Portland's* loss brought a change in the region's maritime technology and design. The vessel's side-wheeler design, with its shallow draft to allow passage up rivers, was declared unfit for ocean voyages. Propeller-driven steamers with deeper draft, more enclosed space, and greater maneuverability replaced paddle-wheelers.

Another vessel lost during the same storm was the *Pentagoet.* The vessel was built in Philadelphia in 1864 and served as a gunboat during the Civil War. It was later converted for coastal trade and used by the Manhattan Steamship Company in its New York to Rockland to Bangor route. Sport divers place the *Pentagoet* on the southern end of Stellwagen Bank; they refer to it as the "Toy Wreck" or "Christmas Wreck" because it carried a cargo of toys.

At least one aircraft crash site is located on Stellwagen Bank. It has been reported that a P-38 Lightning lies on the western edge of the Bank. The cause of this crash remains a mystery.

Silhouetted against red skies, a sailboat moves leisurely across a mirror-smooth sea at sunset. Annually, hundreds of pleasure craft either pass through the Sanctuary en route to New England harbors or journey to Stellwagen Bank for recreational fishing or to observe whales and sea birds. (Alan Hudson)

Over time, as their structure deteriorates and is gradually colonized by marine organisms, shipwrecks are transformed from ruins into underwater habitats. Shipwrecks achieve historical, archaeological, *and* biological value.

Vessel Traffic

The fact that Stellwagen Bank lies near many ports means that large numbers of vessels travel through the Sanctuary every day. International shipping lanes to Boston run directly across the south-central portion of the Bank, and more than 20 million tons of cargo cross the Bank each year. The growing popularity of recreational boating and whalewatching has also increased the number of boats using the Bank.

Kathy Shorr,
Center for Coastal Studies

This heavy vessel traffic can lead to many environmental problems, including collisions with endangered whales, sounds disturbing to marine mammals and other marine life, vessel collisions resulting in cargo spillage and pollution, and disposal of debris into the waters around the Sanctuary.

A zone within the shipping lanes separates inbound and outbound traffic, reducing the possibility of ship collisions. For this reason, a major oil spill in the Sanctuary area is unlikely. Practices such as discharging ship ballast, pumping bilges, and changing engine oil at sea are now illegal; however, these activities do continue clandestinely, contributing to the deterioration of the marine environment.

Whales, Porpoises, and Dolphins

Greatest of all is the Whale,
Of the Beasts which live in the waters,
Monster indeed he appears, swimming on top of the waves
Looking at him one thinks,
That there in the sea is a mountain,
Or that an island has formed, here in the midst of the sea.
ABBOT THEOBALDUS, CIRCA 1022

And God created great whales. . .
—*Genesis 1:21*
Unrivaled in size by any other animal on earth, the blue whale may reach lengths of more than 100 feet (31 meters). Its majestic tail flukes span twenty-five feet (7.6 meters). (Richard Sears)

OOKING OUT ACROSS A SMOOTH SEA, stirred only by light swells or the occasional splash of a sea bird knifing through the water after a fish, you might not believe that thirty-ton creatures live in the depths of the dim, cool sea below. But just meters from the surface, a humpback whale lingers, appearing as an apparition from the deep. Slowly the mountainous form heaves itself above the surface. Water drains in torrents from its broad back and sluices back into the sea. Overhead, the

With fish flying in all directions, a lunge feeding humpback whale explodes through the surface. The immense quantity of prey consumed is converted into blubber, which provides a thick layer of insulation in cold water and the necessary energy stores for long-distance migration. (Bob Bowman)

visible rush of warm, moist air hangs like a cloud with the humpback's first exhalation.

A close, spine-tingling look at this air-breathing relative of the human species rivets our attention and challenges our imagination. This seemingly remote and alien creature lures us briefly into our ancient past. Here two worlds meet—we above the water and they below.

The same watery barrier that separates human from whale also impedes our learning about these mysterious animals. Even a cursory survey of whale literature reveals that, until recently, the majority of information about whales and their habits came from the whaling industry —an industry that made vast fortunes and killed whales by the millions.

In the seventeenth and eighteenth centuries, Middle Bank (Stellwagen Bank) and nearby waters were profitable whaling grounds for whalers hunting the North Atlantic right whale in sight of the Massachusetts coast. Centuries later, the right whale still returns to these rich feeding grounds, as its ancestors have probably done for millennia.

Seventeen species of cetaceans—whales, porpoises, and dolphins—have been sighted within the Sanctuary and in adjacent coastal waters. Some species occur regularly, using the productive habitat for feeding, nursing, resting, and perhaps even breeding. The list of residents and visitors includes five species of large endangered whales: the blue whale, finback whale, sei whale, humpback whale, and the critically endangered North Atlantic right whale. Seasonal appearances of the minke whales, the smaller porpoises and dolphins, and rare sightings of sperm and killer whales also occur within the Sanctuary.

Ancient, Toothed, and Mustached

Herman Melville described the whale as "that spouting fish with the horizontal tail." Contrary to previous belief, however, whales, porpoises, and dolphins are not fish at all, but marine mammals known collectively as cetaceans (from the Latin and Greek words *cetus* and *ketos,* meaning "whale"). Taxonomically, the order Cetacea includes three suborders: the Archaeoceti, or extinct ancient whales, known only from fossil records; the Mysticeti, or "mustached whales," classified as the baleen whales; and the Odontoceti, or "toothed whales," including the porpoises and dolphins.

The origin of cetaceans is still a topic for much speculation, and debate continues among paleontologists as to the true ancestor of modern whales. It is generally agreed, however, that the common whale ancestor abandoned the land for the sea approximately 55 million years ago. Genetic studies suggest that the closest living land relatives of cetaceans are hoofed animals, or ungulates, which include deer, sheep, camels, and the hippopotamus.

Toothed whales, or odontocetes, make up the largest and most diverse group of whales, consisting of about sixty-five known species worldwide. Toothed whales use their teeth to capture individual prey. This group includes smaller species, such as the porpoises and dolphins popularized in aquariums, the beaked whales, and the familiar sperm whale, glorified by Herman Melville in the classic *Moby Dick.*

Baleen whales, or mysticetes, developed along a different evolutionary path. They are toothless and have evolved a feeding apparatus, known as baleen, that filters mouthfuls of small fish or plankton from the water. Six species of baleen whales occur within the Sanctuary. Many, like the humpback whale, make extensive seasonal migrations, feeding in colder temperate waters, like Stellwagen Bank, in the summer and moving toward the tropics for the winter breeding and calving season.

Early Beginnings

From almost their earliest beginnings, whales have inhabited all the world's oceans. Whales have perfected their ability to survive the challenges unique to warm-blooded, air-breathing animals living in the sea.

The ancestors of modern whales adapted to life in the sea in stages, probably to avoid predators and to take advantage of an abundant food source. In the process, many of the physical features associated with their terrestrial relatives were modified. The nostrils migrated from the conventional site at the tip of the snout to the top of the head, forming a single blowhole in the toothed whales and paired blowholes in the baleen whales. With the blowhole(s) in this position, cetaceans can breathe without interrupting their swimming posture. Underwater, a whale can open its mouth without danger of drowning, because the throat and nasal passages are separated so that the air passage opens to the outside only through the blowhole.

Many other modifications have evolved. Over generations, cetaceans lost nearly all their body hair. Instead,

One obvious difference between toothed whales and baleen whales is the blowhole. Toothed whales have a single nasal opening (left), and baleen whales have two blowholes (right). Powerful muscles open and close the blowhole(s), preventing seawater from entering the respiratory passage. (Left: Bill Rossiter. Right: Carole Carlson.)

Below left: *The grapefruit-size knobs on the humpback's head, each containing one or two bristles, are believed to act as sensors.* (Center for Coastal Studies)

Below right: *The paddlelike flippers of this North Atlantic right whale are akin to our forelimbs. The presence of five rows of bones in the flipper supports the belief that the whale's distant ancestor was a five-toed land animal.* (Center for Coastal Studies)

thick layers of fat provide effective insulation. The skin became smooth and rubbery to allow the animals to move through the water with minimal drag. Additionally, the internalization of certain body parts accommodated the streamlined form necessary for smooth forward motion: the teats and genitals were concealed in slits in the body wall, and the external ear disappeared, leaving only a pinhole opening. Forelimbs were transformed into flattened, paddlelike flippers used for steering and diving. Hind limbs disappeared completely, with only two small bones—remnants of the pelvic girdle—embedded in the whale's muscle tissue. And a new feature appeared—a muscular tail stock with horizontally flattened flukes to propel the body through the water.

Is It a Whale, a Dolphin, or a Porpoise?
A dolphin or dorado on a tropical menu is misconstrued as a marine mammal; a scientist is stumped by a fisherman using the local name "rat porpoise" to refer to a dolphin species; and, by the way, what is the difference between a dolphin and a porpoise?

Historically, proper terminology for whales has always been baffling. Collectively, the terms "whale," "dolphin," and "porpoise" all refer to the members of the scientific order Cetacea. But what are the origins of these terms, and when should we use them?

The term "whale" is probably derived from the Norwegian word *hval,* meaning wheel, which describes the animal's motion when diving. "Dolphin" comes from the Greek word *delphys,* meaning womb. "Porpoise" comes from the old English *porpeis,* meaning swine fish (from *porcus,* "pig," and *piscis,* "fish").

All baleen whales, or mysticetes, are referred to as whales, sometimes as "great whales" due to their enormous size. This term, while certainly applicable to the larger members of the group, such as the blue whale and finback whale, which range up to 100 feet (30 meters), is less appropriate for a small species like the 33-foot (10-meter) minke whale, which is exceeded in size by some of the toothed whales.

The odontocetes, or toothed whales, are generally smaller. Among the larger toothed whales, the term "whale" is used to indicate size rather than any zoological affinity, for example, the sperm whale (60 feet or 18 meters) and killer and pilot whales (26 feet or 8 meters). Their smaller toothed relatives (3 to 13 feet, or 1 to 4 meters) are referred to as porpoises or dolphins.

The question remains, what is the distinction between a porpoise and a dolphin? The answer lies in their anatomical features. True porpoises, members of the family Phocoenidae, are generally smaller (under 6.5 feet, or 2 meters) than their dolphin cousins and have a blunt head with flattened or spade-shaped teeth. In contrast, dolphins range in size up to 13 feet (4 meters) and most have a prominent beak with rounded or cone-shaped teeth. Despite classifications, some scientists maintain that all porpoises and dolphins are small whales, period!

In perfect symmetry, a cataract of spray streams from the tail flukes of a humpback whale. "In the tail," wrote Herman Melville in Moby Dick, *"the confluent measureless force of the whole whale seems concentrated." The rear third of the body, called the tail stock, is heavily muscled and drives the tail flukes, which have no skeletal support.* (Robert Nordblom)

THE BLOW

"There she blows!" "She's having her spoutings!"
These phrases were familiar cries aboard the Yankee
whaling ships, upon sighting a whale. Indeed, the
visible and sometimes audible exhalation, or blow,
of a whale, appearing as a puff of steam, has always
betrayed a whale's presence—often fatally in the not
too distant past.

In *Paradise Lost,* John Milton compared the whale
to "a moving land that draws in, and at his breath
pours out a sea." Both poets and whalers have per-
petuated the misconception that whales spout water.
In fact, the blow is most likely produced by the at-
omization of water droplets trapped in the depres-
sion of the blowhole when the whale breathes out.
Just as we see our breath on a cold winter's day, we
see the whale's blow as its warm, vaporous breath
comes into contact with cooler air.

The characteristic shape of the blow (also called
a blast by whalers) is one way to help to identify
whale species. It varies in height and shape depending on the type and size of whale, and the weather
conditions. The height of the blow is its most conspicuous attribute. The 16.5-foot (5-meter) blow of
the finback whale or the 49-foot (15-meter) blow of
the blue whale can be detected at a considerable distance. The right whale and humpback whale blow
reaches 10 to 16.5 feet (3 to 5 meters), and those of
the minke whale and the smaller toothed whales are
very low or not visible. Due to their smaller size,

*The size and shape of the blow can
identify some whale species. This
blow is from a humpback whale.
Whales exchange more air with each
breath than other mammals—up to
90 percent of their lungs' contents,
as compared with 15 percent in
humans. The blow, which appears as
a hazy puff, is produced as warm
exhaled air condenses when it comes
into contact with the cooler air.*
(Alan Hudson)

The North Atlantic right whale, shown here, has a distinct V-shaped spout because the two blowholes are widely separated. (Center for Coastal Studies)

the blow of most toothed whales is momentary and difficult to observe.

The frequency of the blow is related to what the whale is doing. A cruising finback whale may blow and take in a regular series of breaths at the rate of one or more per minute, and then sound or dive for up to fifteen minutes. A humpback whale typically breathes three to five times in a row, perhaps ten to twenty seconds apart, closing its blowholes to seal off its lungs between breaths. Then it may dive for three to eight minutes, though it can remain submerged for more than fifteen minutes. Returning to the surface, it expels roughly 100 gallons (378 liters) of air every time it exhales. Nearly 90 percent of this air is forced out in less than one second.

The Filter Feeders: Baleen Whales

Baleen whales, the largest of the world's animals, feed on some of the planet's most diminutive occupants: small schooling fish or virtually microscopic organisms called zooplankton. Because they are filter feeders, baleen whales are able to harvest enormous quantities of zooplankton from the sea while expending relatively little energy.

Instead of teeth, these whales have a series of thin, long plates, called baleen, embedded in the gum of the upper jaw. A baleen whale's mouth can contain from 250 to 400 of these plates on either side of its huge jaw. These tough, resilient plates are arranged somewhat like the teeth of a comb, hanging one behind the other, less

Sea water cascades over the humpback's bucketlike lower jaw. Gulpers like the humpback whale feed by filtering mouthfuls of seawater and fish, and then forcing the water out through the baleen. A gull dares to dip close to the humpback's sweeping jaws to scoop up any missed opportunities.
(Center for Coastal Studies)

than half an inch (1.27 cm) apart. On each plate, the outer edge facing the water is smooth, while the edge inside the mouth is frayed into fine, bristlelike hairs. The bristles intertwine with those of the adjacent plates to form a dense mat.

The baleen acts like a giant strainer. To feed, the whale opens its mouth wide, taking in large volumes of water and prey. As the whale closes its mouth, it contracts its throat muscles to squeeze the water out through the sievelike baleen plates. The fish and plankton are left behind, caught in the thick barrier of baleen bristles.

The filtration method of each species differs according to their food preferences and distribution of the food source. Most baleen whales are gulpers, taking their food by the mouthful. Around Stellwagen Bank, gulpers include the blue whale, the finback whale, the humpback whale, the minke whale, and sometimes the sei whale, when it feeds on fish. Gulpers have fairly short baleen plates—ranging from six inches (15.24 cm) in the minke whale to about two and a half feet (.76 meters) in the blue whale.

Gulpers are also known as rorquals, from the Danish word meaning "pleated or tubed whale," so named for the expandable ventral pleats extending from chin to belly. The grooved throat expands and contracts like a giant accordion, increasing the mouth capacity during feeding to allow the whale to take in huge volumes of water and food. Fully extended, the pleated throat forms a pouch that holds tons of sea water per mouthful.

Special elastic ligaments allow the whale's lower jaw to accommodate such super-wide-angle bites. In one gulp, a humpback takes in hundreds or thousands of sand lance. When food is abundant, it may swallow more than a ton of food in one day, easily over a million calories! During its six-month feast at the feeding grounds, an adult humpback will gain an estimated 15 to 30 percent of its total body weight.

The food is converted, in part, into an energy reservoir in the form of a thick layer of blubber. This fat reserve will sustain the whale throughout its southward migration in the fall until its return journey to northern seas in the spring.

Some baleen whales are skim feeders, and include the bowhead whale, the Southern right whale, and the North Atlantic right whale, the only representative of this group in the Sanctuary. They do not have ventral grooves. Unlike gulpers, they don't have the need for an expandable throat region since they don't take food by the mouthful. Instead, skim feeders swim through the water with partially opened mouths. Water streams into the front of the mouth and out the sides through the openings between the long baleen plates (six feet or 1.83 meters). Tiny organisms—copepods—are left behind to be swallowed by the whale.

By May and June, Stellwagen's common seasonal residents, including the endangered finback and humpback whales and their smaller relative, the minke whale, have arrived in full force to feast in the nutrient-rich waters of Stellwagen Bank. Humpbacks travel over 1500 miles (2400 km) from the West Indies to Sanctuary waters for a six-month stay while they satisfy their appetites before their return journey south in November or December. In some years there are occasional sightings of blue whales or sei whales. This may correspond to changes in food sources or fluctuations in water temperature. Migration ranges of the blue whale, finback whale, and minke whale remain a mystery.

AN INSIDE LOOK AT BALEEN

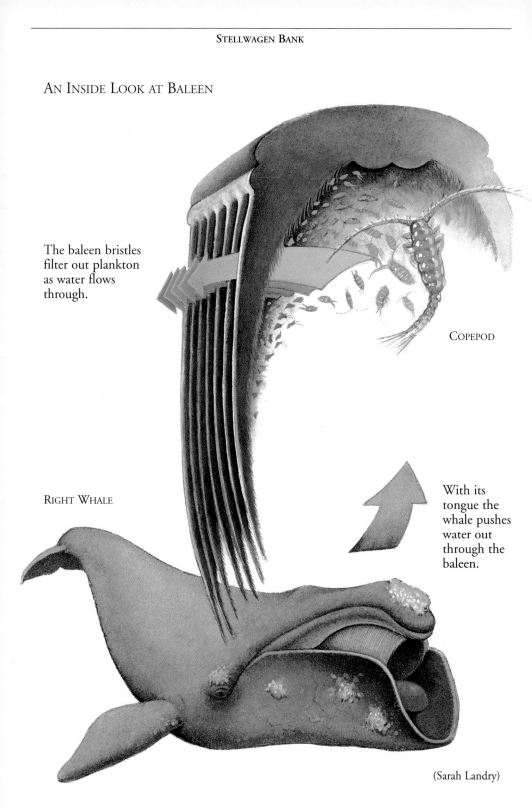

The baleen bristles filter out plankton as water flows through.

COPEPOD

RIGHT WHALE

With its tongue the whale pushes water out through the baleen.

(Sarah Landry)

A GIANT STRAINER

Baleen is made of keratin, the same substance as our hair and fingernails or the horns of animals. From the middle of the nineteenth century, the North Atlantic right whale and other species were hunted for this durable and flexible material, which the Yankee whalers called "whalebone." The baleen, sold for $4.00 a pound at the end of the nineteenth century, was used to make corset stays, venetian blinds, umbrella ribs, sled runners, and buggy whips.

The design of the baleen plates varies among species, reflecting the diet and feeding methods used by each. The North Atlantic right whale's baleen plates reach lengths of up to six feet (1.83 meters). The silky bristles help in capturing massive concentrations of free-swimming copepods. In comparison, finback, humpback, and minke whales have shorter baleen with coarser hairs, which is ideally suited for capturing a varied diet of schooling fish and crustaceans.

Greyhound of the Sea: The Finback

Of a retiring nature, he eludes both hunters and philosophers. Though no coward, he has never shown any part of him but his back, which rises in a long sharp ridge. Let him go, then. I know little of him and neither does anyone else.

HERMAN MELVILLE, *MOBY DICK*

Cruising just below the surface, leaving barely a ripple, a finback whale's sleek, metallic-gray, 60-foot (18-meter) body slips through the sea. Only the air from the blowhole disturbs the smooth sheet of water that begins at the tip of its mouth and rises over its head. The whale makes a final arch before it dives, its back turning wheel-like, a sickle-shaped dorsal fin silhouetted against the backdrop of sky. As the name suggests, this dorsal fin, located nearly two-thirds of the way back from the tip of the snout, is the trademark of the species.

A breaching finback whale is the rarest of the rare. (Center for Coastal Studies)

Clockwise from top: *The curved dorsal fin of the finback has earned it the common name razorback.* (Dave Wiley)

Rolling onto its right side to feed, a finback whale lunges after a school of bait fish. (Center for Coastal Studies)

The light-colored wash sweeping behind the blowholes (the blaze) and the pale V-shaped swirl along the back (the chevron) are used to identify individual finbacks. (Center for Coastal Studies.

Exceeded in size by only the 100-foot- (30.5-meter-) long blue whale, the finback whale may grow to up to 84 feet (25 meters) in the North Atlantic. It is among the fastest of the baleen whales, reaching speeds of up to 12.5 miles (20 km) per hour in short bursts. Astounding speed and maneuverability protected this species from being decimated by the whaling industry until this century, when motorized catcher boats using exploding harpoons began their ruthless hunt of whales worldwide. Currently, the finback whale has been placed on the U.S. endangered species list, but, although they are protected by international agreement, finbacks are still being killed for "scientific" (research) purposes.

The finback's striking asymmetrical coloration pattern is unique among marine mammals. Its lower jaw is a creamy white on the right side but slate gray on the left. Distinctive field marks also include a white blaze on the right side of the head and a buff-colored chevron, a

DEEP VOICES

Along with blue whales and elephants, finback whales share the deepest known voice in the animal kingdom. Finback whale calls are broadcast at extremely low frequency—20 hertz (Hz)—well below the lowest frequency audible to the human ear. This is known as infrasonic sound. Sound travels farther under water than in air, and low frequency sounds travel farthest of all. Undoubtedly, finback whales can hear each other over vast distances. Finback whale sounds have been reported from most oceans that are ice-free and have been recorded in the North Atlantic in both deep and shallow water, including the Cape Cod region.

Irene Seipt, Center for Coastal Studies

The rumbling calls of finback whales are actually pulses of downward-sweeping frequency. A typical pulse lasts for one second, beginning at 23 Hz and ending at 18 Hz. Repetitions of these sound sequences, called "bouts" or "pulse series," may last for thirty-two hours. These bouts coincide seasonally with finbacks' reproductive activity, which is thought to occur from late fall through early spring.

In the world of marine mammals, acoustic display by males during the breeding season is common. Observations of vocalizing finback whales suggest that they are males, since generally it is the smaller finbacks that do the vocalizing, and female finbacks are noticeably larger than the males. In two instances, calling whales have been positively identified as males.

A vocalizing finback barely moves, hovering at a depth of about 160 feet (50 meters), then surfaces slowly. At the surface, the whale takes three to seven breaths over a two-minute period, during which time it usually stops vocalizing. Then the whale submerges slowly, often not even arching its back to dive, and begins its vocal display again.

A vocalizing whale may be in the vicinity of other whales, but it is often separated from quiet whales by 650 feet (200 meters), or more. Generally, one animal vocalizes at a time. If another is heard, the second whale is at least 3 miles (5 km) away.

It has been observed that a vocalizing finback

whale is easily interrupted if another finback whale approaches to within 160 feet (50 meters) or so. Once they separate, the calls begin again. Vocalizations may also stop when the animal is disturbed by the approach of a boat or by any other loud underwater sound.

Finback whale voices are not only low-pitched, they are loud, reaching levels of 160 to 186 decibels (dB) at ranges of 328 to 1640 feet (100 to 500 meters). By comparison, a chainsaw or jackhammer hits 100 to 120 dB, and a jet take-off or shotgun blast is 121 to 145 dB. Our threshold of pain is considered to be 125 dB.

Sensitive recording equipment can pick up finback whales at distances of up to fifty miles (80 km). Who knows how far they can hear one another.

---

pronounced V-shaped band, running down the whale's flank. Scientists photograph the chevron pattern and dorsal fin to identify individuals.

Elusive by nature, the finback is one of the most poorly understood of the great whales. With increased research efforts, an understanding of the finback whale's movements and social behavior is beginning to emerge. Photographic studies of identified individuals demonstrate that finback whales return to the Stellwagen Bank area in consecutive years for feeding throughout the spring, summer, and fall. After giving birth to their 20-foot (6-meter) calves, finback mothers come to the Sanctuary, to replenish their diminished body weights and build up their reserves for the subsequent six-to-ten-month nursing period.

Finback whales eat a variety of pelagic fish such as herring, mackerel, and sand lance. In typical fashion, a finback whale will advance on a school of fish and begin to roll on its side shortly before breaking the surface, simultaneously opening its mouth as it sprints toward the school. This side swimming may facilitate rapid changes of direction and permit the whale to scoop up fleeing fish that attempt to double back past the whale's open mouth. Finback whales are also observed making large circles, 300 feet (91.5 meters) in diameter, before lunging with open mouths. This circling may represent a feeding strategy—perhaps to corral fish or even to disorient prey.

Little Piked Whale: The Minke

The minke whale (*Balaenoptera acutorostrata*) is also called the little piked whale. The latter name may be from the shape of its pointed snout, which one British zoologist observed, "is like that of the Pike fish." Scottish fisherfolk, however, insist that the term *pike* was applied to the high, pointed dorsal fin. The minke's other name is lesser rorqual, since it is the smallest of the rorquals.

Similar in shape to finback whales, the minke whale reaches 30 feet (9 meters) in length. Its small size, fast speed, and tendency to stay at the surface for only short

Reminiscent of bandages, the white flipper patches on minke whales' pectoral fins are unique to the species. (Karen Moore)

A minke's dorsal fin slices through the surface. Today, even though it is the smallest of the baleen whales, the minke is the most hunted whale in the world. (Karen Moore)

periods make it difficult to spot. These elusive behaviors have hindered research, and as a result, little is known about this species.

From a distance, a glimpse of a minke is usually not much more than a flash of its notably curved dorsal fin. Typically, minkes surface briefly, take only a couple of breaths, and then submerge. At closer range, the most recognizable and prominent field mark is the diagonal white band on the dorsal surface of each flipper, making it look as if it were wearing a broad bandage or mittens. No other cetaceans have this characteristic marking.

Research surveys report that minkes are present in the Stellwagen Bank area throughout the year, although they are most commonly seen from March through November. They come to these waters to feed on small schooling fish, primarily sand lance, herring, cod, and mackerel. Following the seasonal movements of these fish, minkes sometimes come close to shore, and, as a result, can become entangled in fishing nets or lobster gear.

In their northern range, minkes are sometimes found in groups of fifteen or more animals where food is present. In Sanctuary waters, however, they more often travel alone or in groups of three or fewer and are difficult to detect. The majority of animals here appear smaller (up to 20 feet, or 6 meters) than the larger cold-water minkes off Canada, perhaps indicating that juveniles populate the Sanctuary area. In other areas, minkes appear to segregate by sex and age classes more than any other baleen whale. Since researchers have not determined the sex or age of minkes in these waters, it is not known whether they segregate here. Mothers with calves are rarely observed in the Sanctuary.

Minke whales are the most common baleen whale in the world. Unfortunately, this world record also gives them the dubious distinction of currently being the most heavily hunted baleen whale. Most of what we know about their population composition, migration, and social behavior has been gained from commercial whalers.

WHAT'S IN A NAME?

We all know Stellwagen Bank's most famous resident as the humpback whale, but this is actually only one of many names that has been given to the animal by different cultures around the world. Most, but not all, of these names are based upon some prominent physical characteristic. The dorsal fin and prominent humped appearance of the whale as it dives has led to its English common name, an association echoed by the same name in other languages: *baleine a bosse,* French; *buckelwal,* German; and *pukkelhval,* Danish, among others. The prominent bumps on the head, called tubercles, prompted other names, such as the Norwegian *knolhval,* "knobbed whale," and the German *Pflockfisch,* "peg fish." One of the most creative names from another language is the Japanese *zatoku-jira,* "whale of the blind people," a reference to the fanciful resemblance of the humpback to one of the blind musicians who roamed the western provinces of Japan carrying a lute on his back and honoring hearth deities. Perhaps the nicest is *vessyl kit,* a Russian name meaning "merry whale."

This profusion of names is certainly interesting, but it becomes a problem when scientists from different countries want to talk to each other about a particular species. For this reason, scientists everywhere refer to the humpback—and any other species—by its scientific name. This is a universally agreed-upon name that is recognized by everyone as referring to only one species.

Scientific names were first developed by the Swedish botanist Carl von Linne, known more commonly by his Latinized name of Linneaus. In the late eighteenth century, Linneaus created the system of classification of living things that underlies all modern taxonomy. Scientific names consist of two parts, and following the tradition begun by Linneaus, they are Latinized. Generally they refer to some physical characteristic of the creature concerned. In the case of the humpback, the features most notable to the zoologist who first described the whale—a German named Borowski—were the whale's very long flippers. Thus, the humpback is

Phil Clapham, Center for Coastal Studies

A humpback raises its sixteen-foot pectoral fin into the air—its Latin name means "big-winged New Englander." The fin is mobile only at the shoulder joint; the rest is stiff and inflexible. (Bill Rossiter)

Three pilot whales swim in tandem. The pilot whale's bulbous head has earned it the common name of pothead. (Gordon Waring, National Marine Fisheries Service)

known among scientists worldwide as *Megaptera novaeangliae,* from the Greek *mega* (big) and *pteron* (wing), a reference to those huge flippers. In full, the humpback is the "big wing of New England" (*novaeangliae*), because the first animal to be scientifically described came from New England waters.

Other cetacean residents of Stellwagen Bank have similarly descriptive scientific names. The finback whale is *Balaenoptera physalus,* "winged whale with bellows." The wing in this case refers to the prominent dorsal fin, and the bellows either to the prominent spout or to the grooves that run along the underside of the animal, which look a little like the pleats of a bellows. The right whale's scientific name today is a sad irony: it is *Eubalaena glacialis,* "true whale of the ice," a reference to the fact that right whales were once abundant in high latitudes along the ice edge. Today, this rarest of all the great whales has long since been eradicated from its former range by hunting. The small minke whale is *Balaenoptera acutorostrata,* "winged whale with a sharp snout." The pilot whale is *Globicephala melaena,* "black rounded head." The commonly seen white-sided dolphin is *Lagenorhynchus acutus,* or "sharp bottle snout."

Since it is possible that the world's oceans are home to as yet undiscovered species of cetacean (a couple of odontocetes are known only from bones, with no sightings of live animals), it is possible that a cetologist may yet have the pleasure of naming a new whale species.

Big-Winged New Englander:
The Humpback

*The humpback . . . the most gamesome and light-
hearted of all the whales, making more gay foam and
white water generally than any other of them.*
HERMAN MELVILLE

In these few lines, Melville aptly describes a breaching
humpback whale (*Megaptera novaeangliae*) as it thunders
out of the water, sending monumental clouds of spray
amid wind and wave. The same wind that threatens
sailors is apparently a jovial playmate to a humpback.
And their playfulness seems contagious; when one
humpback breaches, others often follow suit.

Why would a thirty-five-ton (31,751 kg) whale ex-
pend such energy to hurl itself out of the water? Scientists speculate that it may be a form of communication
or display, or an attempt to dislodge its heavy load of
barnacles. Breaching may even be a method to stun prey.
A humpback's flamboyant acrobatics, whether exploding
in a full-bodied breach, whacking its flukes repeatedly on

*Thirty tons of ponderous grace
thunder out of the water as a
humpback breaches amid a
monumental storm of foam and
spray.* (Robert Nordblom)

Baleen whales are seemingly all mouth. This humpback's cavernous maw, showing its bony pink palate, spans fifteen feet (4.6 meters). As it surfaces through a bubble cloud of green fizz, the distended rorquals—folds of skin that begin at the chin and continue to the belly—balloon out and allow the humpback to take in extraordinary amounts of water and hundreds of fish with every mouthful. (Center for Coastal Studies)

the water's surface, or lifting its massive flippers in a giant salute, make it not only visible but a source of curiosity.

Befitting its scientific name, this whale's long, wing-like flippers may be a third of the total body length. In the North Atlantic, an adult humpback may range from thirty-five to fifty feet (11 to 15 meters) long and weigh thirty to forty-five tons (27,215 to 40,823 kg). Its head is covered with grapefruit-size bumps, known as tubercles, which are really enlarged hair follicles. Yankee whalers called these bumps "stovebolts."

From a distance, humpbacks are easily recognized by their diving behavior. They frequently lift their massive tail flukes—which can span more than twelve feet (3.7 meters)—high into the air. The markings on the underside of the tail flukes are distinctive—no two tail patterns are exactly alike. By photographing these markings and other distinctive features, such as the shape of the dorsal fin or prominent scars, scientists can easily identify individual whales.

Mega-Feasts

Humpbacks appear to have developed feeding techniques that allow them to efficiently trap or concentrate prey. Viewing the feeding behavior of whales is largely limited to the surface. As much as scientists want to understand the function of whale behavior, they can only make educated guesses about what is happening in the dim waters below. Theories abound as to the hows and whys, but so far, all we are able to do is to describe, not explain them.

Bubble Clouds. What we see on top of the water gives an important clue to what's happening beneath the surface. For instance, a circular cloud of green fizz rising to the surface indicates that a humpback has just blown a bubble cloud below a school of fish.

A bubble cloud is formed as a humpback releases millions of tiny bubbles at depth, which then slowly rise to the surface. Some scientists believe that the bubbles concentrate prey by eliciting an anti-predator response, where fish bunch up in order to avoid a predator. The rising air mass of bubbles may conceal the whale's approach or hinder the fishes' ability to escape. Scientists continue to wonder how humpbacks make the bubbles and why.

Bubble Nets. One of the most ingenious feeding techniques is bubble netting. The humpback appears to circle below a concentration of prey while swimming slowly in an upward spiral, releasing streams of bubbles through its blowhole. As the bubbles rise to the surface, they form a circular screen, or net, that may act as a barrier to prey trapped within. The humpback then simply emerges within the net with its mouth open wide, engulfing its catch.

Bubble nets may be as much as a hundred feet (31 meters) across. Often several humpbacks emerge within a net simultaneously. Does one individual construct the net for the benefit of the group, or are the other individuals marauders? Is this an example of cooperative feeding, where they collaborate to construct the net—one for all and all for one? Some scientists believe that humpbacks are able to select the size of the bubbles, making the net a specific "mesh size" according to the prey species, but how they accomplish this geometric design continues to be a puzzle.

Lunge Feeding is seen where prey is abundant at, or near, the surface. How humpbacks detect these massive rivers of small fish is unknown. Once they have located their prey, humpbacks appear to come up toward the surface at a marked angle, with their mouths partly opened. The open mouth spans fifteen feet (4.5 meters), exposing the baleen in the upper jaw. Catapulting jaws cut through the surface, sweeping sideways or almost vertically before the mouth closes and forces out the contained volume of water.

Lobtail Feeding. Feeding styles vary depending on the location, density, and nature of the prey species. A quick smack or two of the humpback's tail flukes on the water generates a shock wave that may even stun the prey below. The crashing slaps create loud sounds underwater, sounds that may frighten fish and cause them to

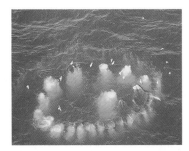

Ingenious hunters, two humpback whales feed inside a bubble net. Nets are formed by one or more circling humpbacks blowing a succession of bubble streams, which rise to the surface. The net apparently corrals the sand lance, allowing the humpback to feast. Hungry sea birds are keen for leftovers. (Robert D. Kenney. Photographed from the MetLife airship.)

A variation of bubble feeding, lobtail feeding is a series of quick flicks of the tail fluke on the surface, before a dive. Underwater, the humpback blows a bubble cloud and then resurfaces where it lobtailed, scooping up quantities of presumably disoriented fish.
(Alan Hudson)

school more tightly. Tight schooling may then cause anoxic conditions—reducing the fish's oxygen supply. Then the humpback makes a steep dive, presumably circles behind the disoriented fish, and engulfs hundreds before they can regroup and swim off. Known as lobtail feeding, this behavior is not practiced by all humpbacks, but there is evidence that the technique is spreading through the population with time. There is also tremendous individual variation in style.

Irene Seipt, Center for Coastal Studies

SAND LANCE

A hushed whale-watching boat floats silently over Stellwagen Bank in thick fog, the passengers a mere breath away from locating a whale by the sound of its exhalation. Suddenly a pattering sound fills the saturated air as the surface of the sea explodes with panicked small fish flinging themselves out of the water. This is their last desperate attempt to escape the wide-open mouths of four humpback whales.

It is a feeding frenzy on Stellwagen Bank, and the main item on the menu is sand lance (*Ammodytes americanus*), large numbers of them. Driven to the surface by lunging whales, the fish become accessible to birds that cannot dive to the depths where the fish often school.

Avoidance behavior in sand lance must be well practiced. Not only are they pursued by many creatures, they are eaten in many forms—as eggs, larvae, and adults. It seems incredible that enough sand lance (also known as sand eels) survive to sexual maturity (at least two years). Each female spawns once a year, producing twenty-three thousand eggs, pri-

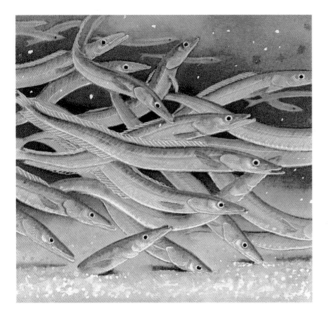

Stripes of steel blue iridescence swim in eel-like fashion over a sandy bottom. These dense schools of sand lance are a preferred staple for a long roster of marine predators. Sand lance have a habit of digging into the sand several inches deep, tunneling their way with their sharp-pointed snouts. (Sarah Landry)

marily during December and January. The eggs are demersal (attached to the sand substrate) and hatch when the water temperature drops to forty-eight degrees F (8.88 degrees C) or lower. The larvae remain in the plankton stage for one to three months, growing approximately half an inch (1.27 cm) per month. One- to three-year-olds dominate the population, but sand lance can live to be five years old, reaching six inches (15. cm) in length. Sand lance have the habit of burrowing into loose sand, earning them their descriptive common name. Their extremely pointed snouts enable them to slide rapidly into the sand, where they lie to escape predation, rest at night, and hibernate in the winter after spawning. Stellwagen Bank, where the sand substrate is aerated by strong currents, has ideal conditions for sand lance.

The preferred prey of sand lance are copepods. These are small ocean crustaceans, flealike in size and appearance, related to shrimp. The planktonic copepods are primarily at the mercy of ocean currents, but they do move up and down in the water column depending on the amount of light. They tend to move toward the surface on gray days and at night, and toward deeper water in bright mid day. Feeding sand lance follow the copepods, and because they use vision to locate their food, light controls when and where sand lance dine.

Sand lance populations fluctuate from year to year depending partly on water temperature and circulation but primarily on the size of predator populations. In 1986 and 1987, for example, the sand lance population on Stellwagen Bank crashed as some of their predators—herring and mackerel—increased. This fact will always keep fishermen challenged, sea birds on the wing, whales gathering or scattering, and whale watchers listening.

Scylla: One Whale's Tale

Phil Clapham, Center for Coastal Studies

It is the month of February in the year 1980. In the warm tropical waters of the West Indies, an adult female humpback whale has just mated with a male who, like her, has traveled to this location from the cold, high-latitude waters of the western North Atlantic. The male has probably had to fight other males for the chance to mate with this female, and he may remain with her for a few more hours, making sure that no other male has access to her during the remaining time that she is fertile. Shortly afterward, the male deserts her to seek other mates. The female, now pregnant, begins the long return migration to her ancestral feeding grounds in the Gulf of Maine.

Three or four weeks later, she has arrived back home and is sighted by whale researchers, to whom she is known as Istar. This is not the first time that they have witnessed her return to the productive waters off Cape Cod; she was first observed in 1977, and since then is known to have had two calves. Istar begins to feed on the small fish that are her primary diet. She has arrived earlier than most other humpbacks from this population, and will remain longer into the coming fall, packing on as much weight as possible in order to prepare for

Spring is an exciting time in the Sanctuary as the year's crop of new mothers and calves arrive. A humpback calf will nurse for about six months, gaining almost 100 pounds a day. (Deborah Glöckner-Ferrari. Photographed under federal permit from the National Marine Fisheries Service.)

the great demands that lactation will bring following the birth of her calf. Istar wanders widely in her search for food. She will linger on Stellwagen Bank for a while, then travel across the Gulf of Maine to the many banks off Nova Scotia. Perhaps she will even venture farther north toward Newfoundland.

By fall, the fetus in her womb is growing at a rate much faster than that of any terrestrial mammal. In the final two months of the year-long pregnancy, it will double in size. By November, Istar is fat from months of feeding. Responding to some unknown environmental or internal cue, she once again turns south and swims slowly toward the Caribbean. There, in February 1981, she will give birth to her third calf, a daughter.

The birth is quick, and the healthy calf is able to swim immediately. Twelve feet (3.66 meters) long and 1500 pounds (682 kg) at birth, she soon learns to nurse, taking the fat-rich milk from her mother and gaining a hundred pounds (45.45 kg) per day. For a few weeks she will wander the waters of the West Indies, hearing the haunting songs of lone male humpbacks echoing through the deep. Often, she and her mother will travel with an adult male who accompanies them in the hope that Istar will once again come into heat and mate. But this year she will not.

In late winter, Istar and her daughter begin the long trek across open ocean routes to the Gulf of Maine. On Stellwagen Bank, the same researchers are delighted to see this familiar whale with a new calf, whom they name

Scylla. It has been two years since Istar's last calf, and this interval provides another valuable piece of the emerging picture of humpback whale reproduction.

Scylla takes nothing but her mother's milk until she is about six months old, when she begins to learn how to catch the fish and krill that will be her principal food for the rest of her life. Four months later she is weaned, and shortly afterward she separates from Istar. In coming years, they will often pass each other on their endless wanderings around the Gulf of Maine, but will spend little time traveling together; once broken, the bonds between mother and daughter are rarely reestablished.

In the succeeding years, Scylla returns faithfully to the waters off Cape Cod. In 1986, she is five years old and now sexually mature. That winter, she mates for the first time. Following the pattern of her mother and hundreds of other female humpbacks, she returns, pregnant, to feeding grounds in the north.

It is the spring of 1987, and Scylla has arrived on Stellwagen Bank with her firstborn calf, Tatter. The researchers are jubilant, for this is only the fourth time that a third-generation calf has been documented in any humpback whale population, and they are beginning to realize that previous estimates of the age at which humpbacks attain sexual maturity—estimates derived from animals killed by the whaling industry—are seriously wrong. The calf nurses just as Scylla herself did only six years before, and travels widely around the Gulf of Maine during the summer, always near her mother's side.

Late in the year, tragedy strikes. Tatter, now weaned and independent, eats mackerel whose livers are tainted by a toxin caused by Red Tide. Like many other whales in the Gulf of Maine, the calf dies as a result of this poisoning. Its body washes up on a beach of Cape Cod, where it is examined sadly by the same researchers who only weeks earlier had been delighted by the young animal's playful behavior in the waters of Stellwagen Bank. It is a somber ending to a story that began with much promise in the Caribbean less than a year before.

Scylla, however, survives. The coming years will bring many migrations to and from the West Indies and a new calf every two or three years to delight the researchers in the Gulf of Maine. Occasionally, Scylla will encounter her mother with a new calf of her own.

How long will Scylla live? We do not know. Perhaps as long as sixty years, but more probably around forty. Soon, perhaps, she will become a grandmother herself as one of her daughters matures and brings her own first calf back to the waters of Stellwagen. And so, the matri-line that began generations before Istar, and millennia before the birth of the researchers who named her and her descendants, will continue, extending into a long and distant future.

GOING FOR A SONG

In biological terms, a song is any series of sounds produced in a stereotyped pattern. Even the two-note chirp of a cricket is technically a song because it follows such a pattern. The great variety of bird songs is familiar to us all. Humpback whales also sing, and their songs are among the most complex in the animal kingdom.

Phil Clapham, Center for Coastal Studies

A humpback song consists of a series of phrases repeated to form what is called a theme. There may be up to nine themes in a song, sung in a particular order. Songs last anywhere from a few minutes to half an hour, and whales have been known to continue singing uninterrupted day and night. Songs are very loud, and can be heard in deep water over at least twenty-five miles (40 km). All of the whales in a given population, such as in the West Indies, sing the same song, which is different from that being sung elsewhere, such as off Hawaii. The song changes progressively over time; two songs recorded a couple of years apart in the same area can be radically different in form and content. Yet remarkably, somehow all of the whales manage to keep up with these changes. How this happens—whether it occurs entirely by cultural transmission or involves some element of an innate pattern—remains one of the larger mysteries about this fascinating whale.

This whale, Trunk, is one of the few individuals known to have sung on the summer feeding grounds in the Sanctuary. Most humpback singing occurs on the whales' winter breeding grounds off the West Indies. Trunk's almost completely white tail flukes are easily recognizable. (Center for Coastal Studies)

Singers are usually lone males. It seems clear that one of the principal functions of humpback whale song is as a breeding advertisement; in this, as in so many other things, humpbacks are no different from the males of a host of other species ranging from frogs to birds. The song may also serve to maintain a spatial separation among males. It has even been suggested that, like the roaring of red deer, it acts as an acoustic cue to stimulate and synchronize estrus in females.

Singing occurs primarily, but not exclusively, on the winter breeding grounds in the tropics. In the spring of 1982, scientists were amazed to hear a humpback singing on Stellwagen Bank. This was initially passed off as an anomaly, but the next few years brought more recordings of song from Stellwagen, in spring, in fall, and even in the summer. The occurrence of this behavior at a time when the whales are not breeding complicates the debate concerning song's function.

Whatever their purpose, humpback whale songs remain one of the most beautiful features of the world's vast oceans.

Dim Shadows of the Past: The North Atlantic Right Whale

On Stellwagen Bank, only a few miles from the civilized world, you have the opportunity to come face to face with the critically endangered right whale, one of the rarest animals in the world—a privilege that may not be possible for your great-grandchildren. Regrettably, today's glimpses of right whales feeding, caring for their young, or engaging in social interactions are but dim shadows of what went before. Just a few centuries ago, thousands of right whales lived in these waters.

A Face Like No Other

The North Atlantic right whale is easily distinguished from other baleen whales likely to be seen on Stellwagen Bank. Distinctive features of this species include the absence of a dorsal fin, a V-shaped spout, a highly arched mouth, lack of throat grooves, and broad, paddle-like flippers. The smooth, clean lines of the tail flukes may

span more than eighteen feet (5.5 meters) and are often lifted high out of the water when diving.

A right whale's head is mottled with large, light-colored growths called callosities. The location of these roughened skin patches corresponds to the location of facial hair on humans—above the eyes, on the jaw and chin, and below the nostrils. Callosities are several inches thick and offer anchorages for whale lice—cyamids—which make the roughened patches appear orange or whitish-yellow. The shape and location of these patches differ for each right whale, allowing scientists to identify individual whales by analyzing photographs of the callosity patterns.

The North Atlantic right whale's face is mottled with whitish callosities—raised patches of thickened skin that are often several inches thick. The central callosity on the upper jaw was called the bonnet by old-time whalers. The pattern of callosity patches is unique to each whale, enabling scientists to distinguish one right whale from another. (Bob Bowman)

Skim Feeding

The right whale's fifty-foot (15-meter), seventy-ton (63,502-kg) bulk requires extraordinarily large amounts of prey to meet its high energy needs. The whale uses a specialized feeding style called skim feeding to collect the massive quantities of zooplankton that periodically concentrate in the surface layers of the water column. The convoluted patterns that the right whale makes when

A North Atlantic right whale feeds by skimming open-mouthed through a plankton patch. No larger than a grain of rice, tiny zooplankton are the mainstay of the right whale's diet. Dense swarms of zooplankton may be many meters across yet only a couple of centimeters thick.
(Center for Coastal Studies)

harvesting the areas of densest food suggest that the animal exploits plankton patches with calculated efficiency. When the whale is skim feeding, researchers are provided with an unusual opportunity to observe right whale foraging behavior.

Plankton patches are made up of dense swarms of protein-rich copepods. These patches can cover an area many meters wide, and yet may be only a few centimeters thick. While feeding at the surface, right whales swim slowly through prey patches with their mouths open, skimming the surface layer with a steady plowing motion. During a feeding bout, a right whale nods its head up and down every few minutes, which suggests that the whale is dislodging the millions of copepods from the thick baleen mat prior to swallowing.

The "Right" Whale to Catch

The *Mayflower* Pilgrims remarked that one could almost walk across Cape Cod Bay on the backs of whales, such was their relative abundance in the early seventeenth century. New England whalers were keen observers of right whales, noting that they were slow swimmers and easy to approach. To old-time whalers,

ZOOPLANKTON—NATURE'S SOUP

*[The right whale] lives cleanly because people say it
does not eat any food except darkness and rain. And
when it is caught and its intestines are opened, nothing
unclean is found in its stomach.*

From a thirteenth-century Norwegian text

This passage is an extraordinary description of the
feeding habits of the North Atlantic right whale.
Unbeknownst to the author, the water that the
whale appeared to be swallowing was filled with tiny
animals—most of them no larger than a rice grain.
These small organisms, called zooplankton, feed vo-
raciously upon small plants called phytoplankton.

In the early spring on Stellwagen Bank, phytoplankton blooms are followed by an explosion of
zooplankton, which in turn becomes an abundant
food source for the grazing right whale. With its exclusive diet of small, planktonic crustaceans, mainly
copepods (in particular, *Calanus finmarchicus*), the
right whale is the only true plankton-eating whale
that regularly occurs off the Massachusetts coast.

this once-abundant, now-rare species was an easy target.
The great value of their six-foot (1.83-meter) baleen
plates, the high oil yield obtained from their thick blubber layer, and the fact that they floated when dead inspired their name—they were the "right" whale to catch.

The pre-hunting population of North Atlantic right
whales may have been as many as eighty thousand animals. Right whale hunting was begun in Newfoundland
by the Basque whalers in the 1500s. Between twenty-
five thousand and forty thousand whales were killed
within a century. By 1750, the stocks off the North Atlantic coasts were severely depleted and the animal was
in danger of becoming extinct.

Today, it is estimated that fewer than 300 North
Atlantic right whales survive. Although this species has
been protected since 1935, the population appears to be
in a continued decline.

Residents

North Atlantic right whales are resident in Cape Cod Bay and within the adjacent Sanctuary boundaries primarily from January through early May. Foraging for copepods is their main activity while in the area. Late in the spring, mothers visit the bay with their newborn calves. As many as thirty to forty individual right whales are in the area yearly. More than half of the total population has been sighted in the area since studies began in the 1980s.

In summer, right whales make their way northward to feeding grounds in the colder waters off Maine, New Brunswick, and Nova Scotia. These areas are also important mating and nursery habitats. On their return migration in October and November, they are rarely sighted on Stellwagen Bank as they make their southerly trek to their winter grounds. The southern extent of their range in the waters off Georgia and Florida is their only known calving ground.

Teetering on the Brink of Extinction

Why, after almost sixty years of protection from hunting, has there been no significant increase in the population of North Atlantic right whales? There are several possible explanations. Scientists believe the diminished size of the population results in inbreeding and thus a limited gene pool. One negative consequence of inbreeding may be a diminished resistance to disease. The species' low birth rate—one calf every three or four years—is also a

The elegant tail flukes of a North Atlantic right whale, some twenty feet across, lift above the surface before it dives, or sounds.
(Center for Coastal Studies)

That Whale's My Home!

Whales have become the metaphor for humanity's ability to overexploit, and even destroy, the natural resources of the world. What few people realize is that each individual whale is like an island ecosystem, hosting a variety of external critters such as cyamids (whale lice), barnacles, and diatoms. They also host internal ones, such as tapeworms, intestinal worms, gut bacteria, and viruses.

The creatures dependent upon cetaceans have probably evolved in ways similar to those in terrestrial ecosystems. Some have specialized into niches where they can only live upon a single species, thus tying their evolutionary survival to the fortunes of their hosts. Others are generalists, able to thrive in a variety of mammal species in all parts of the ocean.

Little is known about the relationship between whale hosts and the many tiny creatures who depend on them. Certainly some gut bacteria are essential for digestion in marine mammals. It's possible that whale lice actually serve as cleaners for whales. Even less is known of the life cycles of most animals that live in, or on, whales and dolphins.

A few researchers have used the parasites found in several whale species to study whale ecology and life history. Studying the changes in the distribution and abundance of external parasites on large whales may answer questions about whether animals mix with other species, as well as giving clues about an individual animal's health and about whale migrations.

Because some of the host marine mammal species are so endangered, so are several of the parasite species. For example, the right whale is host to two species of whale louse—*C. erraticus* and *C. gracilis*—found nowhere else. Studies suggest that each adult right whale can carry up to a million lice. These remarkable and abundant creatures are nevertheless severely endangered, because so few habitats (i.e., right whales) are left for them.

These ecosystems dependent on each whale may be thrown out of balance because of environmental stress. Such stresses could include normal diseases,

Scott D. Kraus, New England Aquarium

Whale lice, or cyamids, make their homes in the folds around the eyes, flippers, and wartlike callosities. These half-inch hitchhikers seem to cause little damage to their hosts. (Scott Kraus)

injuries from predators or competitors, or human activities. Field observations suggest that injured whales do show increased levels of external parasites, suggestive of either slower swimming speeds or a debilitated immune system.

Studies on the natural ecosystems found in and on marine mammals are needed to determine "normal" states. Deviations from the normal patterns may prove to be effective indicators of environmental stress. What appears initially to be a strange aspect in the study of marine mammals may prove an essential tool to assess the health of whales, dolphins, seals, and their oceanic homes.

factor contributing to the population's slow recovery. Right whales' slow movement (2.5 to 3.7 miles or 4 to 6 km per hour) and their tendency to rest on the surface make them especially vulnerable to collisions with vessels.

Additional pressures on this critically endangered species include fishing gear entanglement (60 percent of the population bears entanglement scars), as well as ongoing habitat degradation. Because North Atlantic right

Two North Atlantic right whales caress and enfold one another with their broad flippers. One individual rolls, exposing its black-and-white belly. It takes two to tango, and whales are no exception. (Center for Coastal Studies)

whales are a highly migratory species, the need to protect their habitat is critical. What are the intricate dynamics between species and habitat that are essential to the recovery of the right whale and to the health of the entire ecosystem? The question challenges scientists to find further explanations and solutions before it is too late.

Toothed Whales

Inquisitive and playful, porpoises and dolphins have been the subject of art, myths, and legends for centuries. The dolphin motif appears on Scandinavian rock carvings that date back to the Stone Age. Greeks believed that the dolphin embodied the vital force of the sea: *thalassa*—water, the source of life. The Greeks deified dolphins. Aphrodite, the goddess of love, rode a dolphin. Italian coins etched with dolphins, symbolizing maritime power, were currency during the Roman classic period. Mariners past and present reiterate the belief that dolphins are the friends of man and that they delight in keeping ships company.

The odontocetes, or toothed whales, include a diverse assemblage of sixty-five or more species of porpoises and dolphins worldwide. This group also includes the larger

Left: *A pair of white-sided dolphins cruise just beneath the surface. Their streamlined form makes them superbly adapted for life in the sea.* (Richard Sears)

Right: *A rare appearance on Stellwagen Bank, this convoy of six female orcas (*Orcinus orca*), or killer whales, travels in synchronized formation, often coming up for air at the same time.* (Carol Danton)

177

toothed whales—the sperm whale, pilot whale, and orca or killer whale.

The majority of toothed whales inhabiting the temperate waters of the Sanctuary are considered to be inshore species, attracted to the area by its rich food supply. Their daily activity patterns, seasonal migrations, and reproductive strategies vary greatly among species.

Eleven species of odontocetes have been sighted in the Sanctuary. The Atlantic white-sided dolphin, the pilot whale, and the harbor porpoise are considered seasonal residents. Their occurrence is associated with the abundance of prey.

The white-sided dolphin is the most abundant small cetacean in the area. Harbor porpoises appear in early spring, following their annual migration, which seems to correspond with herring abundance. In fall and winter, groups of up to a hundred pilot whales appear more frequently in the area, chasing schools of squid and mackerel in inshore waters.

Occasionally killer whales visit Stellwagen Bank in August and September as they follow schools of bluefin tuna. Sporadic glimpses of white-beaked dolphins, bottlenose dolphins, and common dolphins have been noted throughout the year. Sightings of Risso's dolphins and striped dolphins have also been recorded, although they are considered rare visitors, preferring deeper and more open waters. There have been several sightings of belugas, or white whales, but their occurrence is an oddity. Sperm whales, the largest of the toothed whales, have made rare appearances in the region. Sightings are extremely rare since sperm whales are deep-water whales, generally congregating in depths of more than 100 fathoms (600 feet).

A Tooth Is a Tooth Is a Tooth

Unlike most land mammals, whose teeth are differentiated into canines, incisors, and molars, the teeth of odontocetes are all the same shape. Presumably, specialized teeth are not necessary for toothed whales since they do not use their teeth for ripping, crushing, or chewing, but only for seizing prey.

The teeth of some whales may take curious forms. The single, spiraled tusk of narwhals and the teeth of most beaked whales erupt only in males, and may function as a sexual display. With age, the teeth of belugas and bottlenose dolphins become badly worn or are shed completely. The sperm whale has teeth only in the lower jaw!

Some toothed whales feed exclusively on fishes or squid, while others are generalists, feeding on a wide variety of animals. The number of teeth varies with feeding habits. Broad-headed species, such as pilot whales, which feed primarily on squid, have fewer teeth than their narrow-headed cousins. White-sided dolphins, and particularly those species with varied diets of small schooling fish and other animals, have a greater number of teeth.

Social Behavior

The fluid motion and lightning speed of a group of dolphins, all moving in perfect synchrony, are a treat to behold. Whether hitching a ride on the bow wave of a boat, sprinting across the water with sudden split-second turns, or engaging in high-spirited leaps and flips, dolphins appear to be engaged in choreographed acrobatics. Their highly coordinated behavior gives us a glimpse into their social systems.

Most dolphins are social mammals that carry out their daily activities within the security and efficiency of a school (or pod). For them, group living can be beneficial. Working cooperatively, the dolphins herd prey more efficiently, ward off predators more effectively, and share responsibilities for their young. There are costs associated with group living as well. Dolphin groups require larger aggregations of prey to feed effectively, and predators may detect groups more easily than they do individuals. Whatever the cost and benefit analysis may be, the fact is that toothed whales are social animals, generally traveling in pods ranging in size from five to thousands of individuals.

Within most mammalian social systems, males and females have different reproductive strategies. Males put

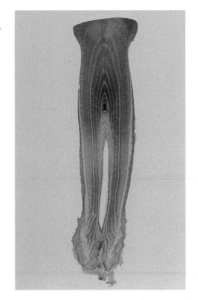

A whale's tooth has growth rings just as a tree does. A ring sequence is created every year—a darker layer and a lighter layer. A porpoise's age can be determined by counting the annular growth rings, starting from the inner pulp cavity (white space).

This tooth is a decalcified and stained section of a sixteen-year-old harbor porpoise killed accidentally in a sink gill net. This is one of the oldest-known harbor porpoises from the Gulf of Maine. Note the very worn down crown. (Andy Read)

A white-sided dolphin mother and her calf swim side by side.
(Bob Bowman)

their energy into securing the greatest number of mating opportunities, while the females' investment lies in the raising of their young. For cetaceans, the basic social unit appears to be a mother-and-calf (matrilineal) group. Mothers are extremely attentive to their calves; pilot whales and sperm whales may nurse their young for more than two years.

Sometimes the social system extends beyond mother and calf. Researchers doing long-term studies off Florida's west coast have observed bottlenose dolphins babysitting—another female, or "aunt," tends the young calf while the mother goes off to search for food. Understanding kinship bonds is an important part of understanding dolphin social systems. However, extensive studies on dolphins' family relationships and behavior have yet to be conducted on Stellwagen Bank.

A Whale's Senses

Underwater, the distinction between taste and smell is less obvious than it is on land. Studies on cetaceans suggest that odontocetes are unable to smell, while baleen whales may have a rudimentary sense of smell. The sense of taste appears to be present in some species. How cetaceans use their senses of taste and smell is unknown.

Cetaceans can see in air as well as water. When handicapped by murky or dimly lit water, their range of vision is restricted considerably. Odontocetes compensate for their less-developed senses of smell, taste, and sight, however, with their extraordinary acoustic sense.

There is considerable debate among researchers as to how cetaceans hear. There are no external ears, only a tiny slit behind the eye. In terrestrial animals, the outer and middle ear are designed to transmit airborne sound to fluid in the cochlea—inner ear. It is suggested that hearing in toothed whales occurs either by sound being transmitted from the skull bones to the inner ear, or by sound being conducted to the inner ear by fat deposits within the lower jaw.

Built-In Sonar

Toothed whales possess an acoustic faculty that allows them to "see" with their ears. But how? Odontocetes have the ability to echolocate by producing clicking sounds and interpreting the returning echo.

The eyes of a dolphin can quickly adapt to intense light at the surface as well as to the twilight world below. (Richard Sears)

Dolphins can observe their surroundings in this manner. For example, they can determine the distance to an object by measuring the time between an outgoing click and its returning echo. It is estimated that their range of acoustic vision is at least 328 feet (100 meters). Like a ship's echo sounder, they can collect general information about water depth, the topography of the sea floor, and whether there are any large objects or animals in the area.

Studies of captive animals suggest that once the dolphin has located a target, the animal emits a series of clicks across a broad frequency band to establish the distance and direction of the target. Once the bearing of the target is determined, the dolphin focuses high-frequency sounds toward the target, which give the most detailed information. For animals in the wild, the echoes received may give many different kinds of information—for example, is it a school of squid or a shark?

High frequencies are absorbed quickly by the water, so they are useful only at close range. As the dolphin gets closer to the target, the clicks come very close together, producing a continuous creaking sound. This short-range sonar may give detailed information about the internal anatomy or external texture of the target. The dolphin may even scan the target by moving its head from side to side in order to receive a broader image, thereby gleaning information about the target's movement and size.

The sensory ability to echolocate is confined to toothed whales. Considering the constraints of a dark

HOW DO DOLPHINS ECHOLOCATE?

1. Sounds travel very fast in water— about a mile (1500 meters) per second. A dolphin might detect a school of fish that is 100 meters away (the length of a football field) in about one-eighth of a second. It takes one-sixteenth of a second for the sound to travel to the fish, and one-sixteenth of a second for the returning echo to travel back to the dolphin.

2. To "see" what lies ahead, a dolphin sends out a high-frequency sound (a click).

3. Some distance away, the sound waves hit an individual fish or a school of fish. The sound bounces back to the dolphin in a returning echo.

4. When sound hits an object with a different density from water, like the air bladder of a fish, a stronger echo signal is reflected.

5. The returning echo provides the dolphin with specific information. For instance, the dolphin may estimate its distance from a "target" by measuring the time interval between the outgoing click and the returning echo.

AIR BLADDER

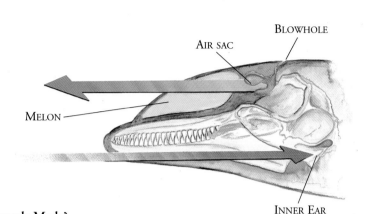

MELON

AIR SAC

BLOWHOLE

INNER EAR

How Are the Sounds Made?

1. The clicking sounds that some toothed whales use for echolocation may be produced in the nasal sacs—the bulges in the nasal passage below the blowhole. Scientists speculate that air forced back and forth past constrictions in the passage may cause vibrations in the nasal sacs and produce the click sounds.

2. The sounds are transmitted forward through a malleable organ in the dolphin's forehead called the melon. The melon is filled with oil of varying density, which some scientists believe may help to focus the sound waves (green arrow), similar to the way a magnifying glass focuses light.

3. The returning echo may not be perceived by the outer ear, which is not in a good position to receive sounds coming from in front of the animal. Some scientists suggest that the returning echoes enter the lower jaw and travel along an oil-filled channel to the inner ear.

KEY
Green arrows = transmitted sound
Orange arrows = returning echo

(Illustrations by E. Paul Oberlander, adapted from *Zoobooks: Whales,* Wildlife Education Ltd., San Diego, Calif.)

ocean, it is not surprising that they have developed such an effective and efficient method to catch food and avoid predators.

Pilot Whales

On a breezy October afternoon, a good eye may see black bulbous heads thrusting above the water's surface in methodical forward movement, or thick black dorsal fins and tail flukes punctuating the water's surface with brief splashes. An assortment of heads, fins, and flukes from ten pilot whales is spotted above the surface; there are perhaps twice as many under the surface, following a different rhythm.

Long-finned pilot whales (*Globicephala melaena*)—also known as potheads because of their rounded foreheads or as blackfish because of their coloration—are most often seen in the Sanctuary in September and October. Their common name probably comes from the fact that the whales within a group follow a leader, or pilot.

Six long-finned pilot whales swim together. Toothed whales are efficient hunters and often travel in groups, perhaps to herd prey. (John Domont)

From colonial times to the early 1900s, Cape Cod-ders drove schools of potheads ashore for their oil and meat. These drive fisheries were the mainstay of some New Englanders; the whales' bulbous heads contained valuable reservoirs of highly prized oil.

Historically, as well as today, pilot whales commonly stranded on beaches in the Cape Cod region during the fall and winter. Scientists do not know the cause of these mass strandings, although many theories have been suggested. Parasitic infestations of the inner ear may interfere with the animal's ability to navigate. Or, they may follow prey or flee from predators into areas where the slope of beaches renders sonar systems inoperable. Or adverse weather conditions may disorient them. Any or all of these theories could help explain the mass strandings.

Using information provided through whaling records and studies of dead animals on beaches, we are beginning to understand the group structure of pilot whales. Evidence suggests that mature females may act as group leaders, initiating seasonal movements to locate food sources. Group sizes vary, ranging from five to more than one hundred animals, and consist of mixed age classes of males (up to 20 feet, or 6 meters), females (up to 16 feet, or 5 meters), and calves (birth length: 3 feet, or 1 meter).

Our understanding of their social dynamics would be greater if we could study them easily in the wild. With the help of new satellite technologies such as radio-tagging, we are gaining insight into the free-ranging world of whales. In 1987, radio tags on three pilot whales off Cape Cod showed that one whale swam an average of 50 miles (80 km) a day, or 2 miles (3.3 km) an hour. Daytime dives lasted from six to nine seconds. Night dives were longer and deeper, probably reflecting the whales' feeding habits. Satellite monitoring of cetaceans promises to provide basic information on pilot whales' movement and dive patterns, but also on such factors as temperature and currents, which influence how they locate and capture prey. As important, satellite tracking of their migration ranges will define their preferred habitats, which are critical to their survival.

NO AIR DOWN THERE

All whales are skilled divers, but, being mammals, they must return to the surface periodically to breathe. Marine mammals must obtain sufficient oxygen during the brief period when they are at the surface to last the duration of their dive. A skilled human diver may hold his or her breath for two and a half minutes, a hippo for fifteen minutes, and a beaver for twenty minutes. By contrast, a sperm whale can remain under the surface for more than two hours.

How do whales stay underwater for so long? Do they have a larger lung capacity? Proportionally, the lung volume in whales is small (1 to 3 percent of the body) in comparison to land mammals (3 to 7 percent). So how do they manage to stay underwater so long?

Although whales breathe less frequently than land mammals, they inhale more air in a shorter period of time. It has been estimated that an inhaling whale may fill up to 90 percent of its lung capacity during each respiration. By comparison, humans fill up only 15 percent. Large whales are able to take down over 500 gallons (2270 liters) of air. The amount of time spent underwater varies greatly among species. A large whale can hold its breath for more than an hour, while dolphins and porpoises make short, frequent dives, coming to the surface every few minutes to breathe.

Whales have increased their capacity to store oxygen not simply by enlarging lung capacity but by modifying the circulatory system and chemistry of the muscles. The concentration of hemoglobin, the oxygen-carrying pigment in red blood cells, is considerably higher in marine mammals (60 percent) than in land mammals (35 to 45 percent). Another oxygen-carrying pigment, called myoglobin, is also present in all mammalian muscles. The quantity of myoglobin in cetaceans is up to ten times higher than in land mammals, so that on diving, the muscles take a large supply of oxygen with them. But when we add up all the oxygen stored in a whale's lungs, blood, and muscles, we still find that the oxygen stores are inadequate for the known duration of submersion. A significant part of the puzzle is missing—how do these diving animals reduce their oxygen use?

Research on diving animals, including whales, ducks, sea turtles, and seals, shows a profound slowing of the heart beat, a phenomenon known as bradycardia, also called the diving response. Slower heartbeat is accompanied by a redistribution of blood flow, so that only essential organs such as the brain and heart are supplied with oxygenated blood during dives. Blood supplies to other organs—such as the stomach, kidneys, and muscles—may almost cease. Whales can reduce their oxygen consumption by slowing their heartbeat to about one-third of the usual rate and by shutting down blood flow to all but the most critical organs. Although muscles are deprived of their hemoglobin supply, it is augmented by enriched myoglobin stores.

Whale muscles can also function longer without oxygen—anaerobically—than those of land mammals. Unlike us, whales do not seem to suffer from the cramp that results from the build-up of lactic acid, a by-product of respiration.

White-Sided Dolphins

While numerous species of baleen whales make appearances on Stellwagen Bank, only one toothed whale occurs regularly—the Atlantic white-sided dolphin (*Lagenorhynchus acutus*).

Mason Weinrich, Cetacean Research Unit

The Atlantic white-sided dolphin is typically six to eight feet (1.8 to 2.4 meters) in length and weighs just over 200 pounds (90 kg). The species' name comes from a striking whitish-yellow stripe that runs the length of the body on the animal's flank. Apart from this stripe, its coloration pattern is typical of many offshore dolphins —black above and white below. This pattern, called countershading, is believed to have evolved to conceal the dolphin's movements from its predators. In the marine environment, the dark color of the back blends with the darker ocean when viewed from above. The lighter abdomen blends with the bright ocean surface when viewed from below the dolphin.

Named for the striking whitish-yellow stripe on their flanks, white-sided dolphins are vigorous swimmers and willing bow-wave riders. (Center for Coastal Studies)

White-sided dolphins are found only in the North Atlantic, ranging as far north as Norway. Males are slightly larger than females, as is true for most odontocete species. Nicknamed "jumpers" by Newfoundland fishermen, white-sided dolphins occasionally ride the bow waves of ships. They frequently associate with long-finned pilot whales and often feed among finback whales. Their prey species include a variety of fishes, such as herring, sand lance, and squid.

Like most dolphins, Atlantic white-sided dolphins are highly social animals. There are occasional sightings of groups containing only a few individuals, but most pods number between twenty-five and one hundred animals. Larger groups are sighted between May and October. By August and September, groups of one to two hundred are not uncommon. These larger superpods are not stable groups, but may be made up of smaller cohesive subgroups that join and leave the superpod.

While we know little about the composition of Atlantic white-sided dolphin social groups, we do know that many stable dolphin groups are composed of related females and their offspring—both young calves and older juveniles—and several unrelated adult males. These adult males may not stay with any female/young group for long.

Like the larger whales, dolphins have been photo-identified in New England for a number of years to study their group dynamics. Nicks or scars on the dorsal fin are often used to identify individuals, but not every individual has a unique mark. Instead, representative individuals who do have distinctive marks, such as the twenty partial or total albino dolphins, are photographed to give clues about the population as a whole.

These photo-identification studies indicate that Stellwagen Bank is a transient feeding site for many dolphins. Groups of dolphins are reported throughout the winter, with large numbers of dolphins remaining in the area for about three weeks in April.

White-sided dolphins virtually vacate the Stellwagen region between mid-May and early July. By August, sightings become more regular. Individuals travel through the area but remain only for brief periods. Every so often, a dolphin photographed in the spring is sighted in the summer or early fall as it passes through the area again. The same dolphins photographed on Stellwagen Bank have been seen on Georges Bank and off the southern Maine coast, indicating that they cover a wide range. They may move inshore during the colder months, but no clear migratory pattern has been discovered yet.

THE BENDS

Sperm whales may dive to depths of more than 8200 feet (2500 meters), remain underwater for up to two hours, and then rapidly ascend to the surface. How do they, and other cetaceans, withstand the stresses of deep and prolonged dives?

For a scuba diver to reach depths greater than his breath-holding endurance will allow, he breathes compressed air. This is necessary because the air pressure within his lungs must equal the pressure of the water around him—if it were less, his chest would be crushed by external pressure.

As water pressure increases with increasing depth, more and more of the nitrogen in the air he breathes is dissolved into the diver's blood. If the diver rises too quickly from a deep dive, nitrogen bubbles form in the blood cells and tissues—this is similar to the bubbles of carbon dioxide released in a soda can when the top is taken off and the internal pressure is rapidly released. The nitrogen bubbles can stop the flow of blood and cause a gas embolism, in which case the diver suffers crippling pain, paralysis, or even death. This condition is known as the bends.

How do whales avoid the bends, or the build-up of nitrogen bubbles in their bloodstreams?

Unlike human scuba divers, the whale takes down only the air contained in its lungs and air passages. Therefore, the whale is not receiving a constantly fresh supply of nitrogen while submerged. With increasing pressure, the air in the lungs and respiratory passages is compressed, and the whale's lungs and windpipe partially collapse. Much of the compressed air rushes into the nonabsorptive passages in the whale's head. Since the air is removed from the lungs and respiratory passages little nitrogen gets dissolved in the blood and tissues. With this adaptive physiology, the whale can dive safely and thus avoid the high nitrogen concentrations in the blood associated with the bends.

Harbor Porpoises

The harbor porpoise (*Phocoena phocoena*) is the most abundant cetacean in the Gulf of Maine during the summer, rivaled only by the white-sided dolphin. Although these porpoises frequently make appearances in Boston Harbor in April and May, sightings on Stellwagen Bank are few. Generally, a sighting is merely a quick blip of heads and some splashes at the surface—but from quite a distance, as this coastal species rarely approaches boats.

The smallest of the cetaceans in the North Atlantic, the adult harbor porpoise has a six-foot- (1.7-meter-) long, compact body that is built to dive. Tagging studies indicate that they dive to depths of 741 feet (226 meters), feeding on schooling bottom fish such as silver hake and herring. While traveling, they surface frequently to breathe (up to six to eight times in a row at one-minute intervals). Their dives last about five minutes. As a species, harbor porpoises are quite mobile, easily traveling 31 miles (50 kilometers) a day.

Harbor porpoises catch herring and other small schooling fish, consuming up to 30 to 40 times their body weight each year. Like all porpoises, they have

A harbor porpoise is gently lowered into the water, being released from a herring weir in the Bay of Fundy, Canada. A small plastic tag attached to the triangular dorsal fin will allow future identification. About 100 animals are tagged each year. (John Wang, Grand Manan Whale and Sea Bird Research Station)

spade-shaped teeth and no distinctive beak. In comparison to some marine mammals, their life span is relatively short, only about 17 years. Unlike dolphins, female porpoises are larger than males. They reach sexual maturity at three years of age, after which they give birth to a single calf every year, generally in May. Pregnancy lasts for almost eleven months, with mating following in June. Calves are about 30 inches long (75 cm) at birth, weighing about 12 pounds (5 to 6 kg). Cetacean calves are generally larger, relative to the size of the mother, than the offspring of most land animals. Larger body size means a higher ratio of mass to surface area, thereby minimizing heat loss in their underwater habitat.

Swimming close to shore in groups of 15 to 30 animals, harbor porpoises are often entangled in fishing gear. Although we know that their range extends north and east to Nova Scotia, information on their southern range is limited. The only clue comes from winter strandings of yearlings on the North Carolina coast. Harbor porpoises are seen in the Gulf of Maine throughout the spring, summer, and fall, but scientists have no clue as to where they migrate during the winter.

MARINE ENCOUNTERS:
FISHING FOR A SOLUTION

Humans are not the only creatures who make a living from fishing. Beneath the surface, numerous marine creatures are also fishing, often at the same time and in the same location as their competitors on the

Russell DeConti, Center for Coastal Studies

surface. Sometimes encounters between humans and other marine predators are fatal, presenting fisheries managers with one of their most complex problems: how to prevent entanglement of marine mammals in commercial fishing gear.

In the Gulf of Maine, this problem appears when harbor porpoises encounter the gill net fishery. Peak concentrations of harbor porpoises occur within the Sanctuary in April and May as they migrate north along the coast to the Bay of Fundy. Their migratory path brings the porpoise into contact with some of the most heavily fished areas in New England.

Unfortunately, no one knows exactly how harbor porpoises get caught in the gill nets. Fishermen speculate that they may get caught as the nets are set or hauled, or perhaps they are attracted to the nets once a good supply of fish has accumulated in them. Either way, the end result is the same: death by drowning because they can't reach the surface to breathe.

To sustain their population, the number of harbor porpoises dying from all causes each year must not exceed the number of new animals born. Currently, in the Gulf of Maine, the number of animals that die from entanglement in gill nets appears to be at, or above, that number. Due to the limited reproductive capabilities of harbor porpoises, annual losses as low as 4 to 5 percent are considered a threat to the continued viability of the population. Measures for reducing the number of porpoises caught in gill nets include modifying the nets to make them less likely to catch porpoises (or to make it easier for them to escape), attaching noisemaking devices to scare porpoises away, and closing certain areas to gill netting during peak porpoise migrations.

Cooperation among fishermen, fisheries managers, scientists, and the environmental community is critical to finding an acceptable long-term solution to this problem, a solution that both protects the harbor porpoise and allows fishing to continue.

ENCOUNTERS WITH WHALES

I think I could turn and live with animals;
they are so placid and self-contained;
Not one of them is dissatisfied—not one demented
with the mania of owning things.
                    —WALT WHITMAN

WHAT TIME WILL WE SEE OUR FIRST WHALE? How many will we see? Are we guaranteed to see some?" These are just a few of the questions from the mouths of eager whalewatchers as they first set foot on board.

Assurances of sightings and specifics of what to expect are tough to come by, but you can expect an adventure and an exhilarating day at sea. Whether standing out on the pulpit being drenched by salt-spray as the boat plows through two-foot chop, or sitting comfortably and sipping tea, you'll collect plenty of memories.

One of the joys of whalewatching is the search for wild animals in their natural environment, animals that are not limited in their movements by manmade boundaries. At the Stellwagen Bank Sanctuary there is no underwater zoo, no underwater fence.

"Spout! Spout at two o'clock, one-quarter mile!" shouts a deck hand. The finback whale's blow is the visible giveaway of its location. Other telltale signs of a whale may include glimpses of the arching back and dor-

Face to face, a bedazzled whale watcher and a curious humpback whale meet. (Robert Nordblom)

"Footprints," the round smooth patches on the surface of the water, alert a whale watcher that a whale is just below the surface. (K. Moore)

sal fin of the animal as it breaks water, or the splashes produced by leaping dolphins or breaching humpbacks. Hovering sea birds are a good indicator of the presence of small fish—and, perhaps, feeding whales.

Whalewatching: A National Pastime

Whalewatch cruises are conducted over Stellwagen Bank and Jeffreys Ledge from April through October when the greatest concentrations of whales are present. At latest count, more than twenty whalewatch businesses operate from Provincetown and Barnstable, right up to Plymouth, Boston, Gloucester, and Portsmouth, New Hampshire. The whalewatch industry generates more than twenty million dollars annually and carries as many as two million passengers a season. Most of the boats are staffed by naturalists and researchers, who educate passengers about the whales' behavior. Researchers consider the use of whalewatch boats to be one of the most accessible and economic means to collect data on whales in the area. Regardless of whether whalewatching is valued educationally, economically, or esthetically, it surely has become a national pastime.

Oohs and *aahs* burst forth and cameras click away madly when a humpback dives underneath the boat. The spontaneous thrill of seeing a whale more than half the size of the boat is mind-boggling. "Could the whale tip over the boat?" asks a young boy, mesmerized by the approach of a humpback. "It looks like a hippopotamus. How big can it grow?" blurts out another passenger. "Is it going to breach?"

The fantastic shots you see on television are the very best footage available. A whale's daily activity in the wild is vastly different from the acrobatics of trained marine mammals. Our visit to their world is brief; close encounters are a privilege. Our sightings are dictated by their on-the-surface behavior, as well as tight schedules that direct the boats to head back to the harbor to pick up another passenger load.

"It's the best hundred dollars I ever spent on my family," says a satisfied customer. By the end of the trip, it is clear that a whalewatch is an introduction to the many

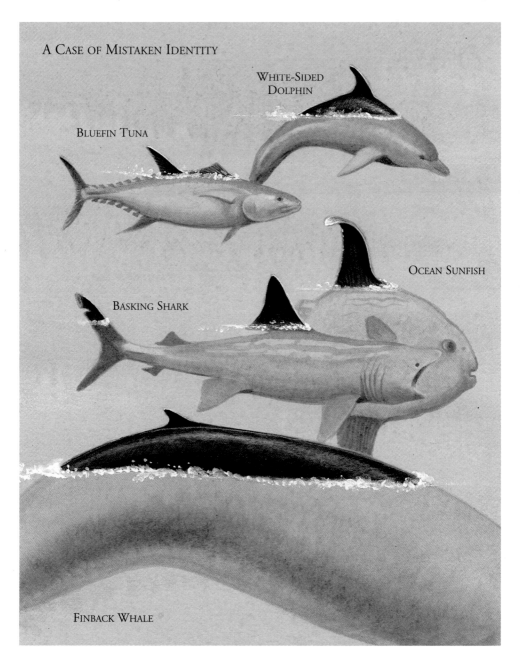

A CASE OF MISTAKEN IDENTITY

WHITE-SIDED DOLPHIN

BLUEFIN TUNA

OCEAN SUNFISH

BASKING SHARK

FINBACK WHALE

It is not unusual to mistake the quick flash of a tuna's dorsal fin, or even the slice of a basking shark's tail fin cutting through the surface, for a dolphin. Many marine animals have dorsal fins of similar size and shape—and often, a quick glimpse of a dorsal fin is all you get. (Sarah Landry)

facets of the Sanctuary—the birds, the fishing boats, the wind and sea, and the whales—all in one package.

As people disembark, comments range from "Boy, this has been the best day of my life," to "I had to eat my words. I didn't think we'd see a thing." Every day is different. "What are they gonna do tomorrow?" You'll have to wait and see.

Al Avellar, the Pioneer

Back in 1959, Al Avellar first toyed with the idea of conducting whalewatching trips out of Provincetown, Massachusetts. As the owner of a charter fishing company, he had seen whales often during his fishing trips. The idea came to him one day when he was captaining his fishing boat. "Everybody was fishing, lines out. But when whales came around, they dropped the poles. I figured, if fishermen would look, there must be something to whalewatching." But at that time, he knew, "People wouldn't pay a nickel to go look for whales."

In the early 1970s, Avellar says, "The newspaper ran front-page stories about cleaning up rivers and harbors, and there were always about a dozen lines about whales becoming extinct." People were becoming environmentally conscious. Avellar still didn't know whether he could convince tourists to spend good money to look for whales. No one on the East Coast had tried the idea, although on the West Coast there had been some success with it.

The decision came down to whether Avellar should go into flounder fishing in a heavy way or take the chance on whalewatching. He opted for "the big fish rather than small fry," and has never regretted it.

On April 15, 1975, he took out his first trip. It was the beginning of whalewatching on the East Coast. "Whalewatching didn't happen overnight," remembers Avellar. "I couldn't give that trip away. I'd stand at the pier and say, 'Would you like to go for a whalewatch?' They'd say, 'No, thanks.'"

"In those days," recalls Avellar, "we'd tell customers to bring their binoculars. They were happy with a distant look at a finback. To help us find whales, we'd promise a

case of beer to the first fishing boat that could radio and tell us where the whales were on the Bank."

From the outset, Avellar hired Dr. Charles "Stormy" Mayo from the Center for Coastal Studies to be a naturalist on board his boat, the *Dolphin*. "I knew it was important to have a scientist on board. It had to be an educational program."

And what about the future? "There are no miracles to whalewatching; the miracles are the whales and the folks' enthusiasm for them. My personal favorite is the first humpback we saw and named—Salt. Salt and her calves keep coming back. It's a great sight."

Humpback whales' tail flukes are like fingerprints—no two are alike. First seen in 1976, Salt is affectionately called the Grand Dame of Stellwagen Bank because she was the first humpback named in the Sanctuary. Named for her all-white dorsal fin, which looks like it is covered with sea salt, she has given birth to six calves since 1980, and in 1992 she became a grandmother. (Center for Coastal Studies)

Occupational Hazards

Carole Carlson

Spring has finally arrived, and with it come humpback whales—spouting, feeding, and frolicking in these northern waters. Their migration from the Caribbean Sea has, once again, brought them to their ancestral feeding grounds. This migration is not always without incident. In fact, there are many hazards involved in twentieth-century travel.

There is still the traditional, or perhaps natural, haz-

197

Black rakelike scars are testimony to past killer whale attacks, probably while Altiplana was still a calf or a juvenile. (Carol Danton)

ard of orca attacks, primarily on humpback calves. The parallel tooth scars on Altiplana's tail indicate that she was a prime target when she was very young. Luckily, Mom was probably close by and protective. Obviously, not all attacks are lethal. Almost 15 percent of the humpback whales from Stellwagen Bank have orca tooth marks on their tail flukes.

Entanglements in fishing gear, such as ropes and nets, are a constant threat to humpback whales. Migrating from the tropics to polar waters, humpback whales may stop to feed in areas with heavy fishing activity, where they can get caught in nets that are fixed to the ocean floor. This is certainly not a new problem, since whales and fishermen have worked the same areas of the ocean for centuries, both taking advantage of rich, productive areas to survive. On the increase, however, are entanglements in discarded or abandoned fishing gear. The high incidence of rope and net scars on the humpback whales of Cape Cod—almost 40 percent—tells us that entanglements are common. As with many of the other hazards that whales face, we have no idea of the number of whales that die from such ordeals.

Also on the increase are boat strikes. Humpback whales often feed in areas of heavy boat traffic—both commercial vessels and pleasure craft. Over the past few years a number of humpback whales have been struck, primarily by small motor vessels. This has been determined by examining propeller scars on whales' bodies

This humpback calf was found on a Chatham beach on Cape Cod. The cause of single strandings is poorly understood, but most necropsied animals appear to have been diseased or unhealthy.
(Center for Coastal Studies)

and reviewing reports, photographs, and videotapes of boat/whale collisions and near-collisions.

Of all hazards, the most threatening of all has been, until recently, the most difficult to see. Now the signs of ocean pollution are everywhere—from the wastes found on our beaches to debris floating offshore to toxic compounds regularly dumped into our oceans. Fish-eating marine mammals, such as the humpbacks, feed close to shore, and their body tissues accumulate contaminants —sometimes to fatal concentrations. As their bodies wash ashore on beaches around the world, the whales are examined. This teaches us much about the state of the world's oceans. From them we learn that the ocean is not so vast, not bottomless. We are beginning to see the effects of our pollution.

Each spring, we are thrilled and amazed to see many of our whales return to Stellwagen Bank, despite the potential problems they could encounter.

Too Close for Comfort

Endangered whales have become the center of attraction for millions of visitors who go whalewatching around Stellwagen Bank each year. Their aim is to see these spectacular animals in their natural environment, diving, feeding, slapping their flippers on the surface, and if they are lucky, breaching or leaping clear out of the water. The educational opportunity provided by professional guided tours has undoubtedly had a positive effect on ef-

Dave Wiley, International Wildlife Coalition

The carcass of this juvenile North Atlantic right whale was found floating in the shipping lanes of Stellwagen Bank. With fewer than 300 individuals left in this critically endangered population, the death of one animal represents a significant hindrance to their recovery. (Center for Coastal Studies)

forts to protect whales. As the popularity of watching whales grows, and as more and more vessels ply the waters in their pursuit, however, concern for the welfare of the whales increases as well.

Federal laws protect whales from harassment and harm. In the Gulf of Maine, federal guidelines specify minimum approach distances to reduce the likelihood of a vessel striking and injuring a whale and to keep too many vessels from crowding around a given animal. The effectiveness of these measures depends upon voluntary compliance.

The issue of how close is too close—and, conversely, how far is too far—has emerged as one on which there is little agreement. Common sense tells us to maintain a reasonable distance from whales to allow them to move about freely and stay unharmed. But what is a reasonable distance?

The Gulf of Maine's whalewatching guidelines, provided by NOAA Fisheries, suggest a Close Approach Zone beginning 100 feet (30.5 meters) from a whale and extending out to 300 feet (91.4 meters). Within this zone only one vessel is allowed. This is surrounded by a Stand-By Zone, from 300 feet (91.4 meters) out to 600 feet (183 meters), where other vessels await their turn for a closer look. Beyond the Stand-By Zone, out to one quarter mile (402 meters), a Whale Awareness Zone is recommended.

Some whales appear to ignore boats altogether, while others appear curious and will even come over for a

Scars left from a boat's propellers on this humpback whale are testimony to a boat strike. (Alan Hudson)

closer look. At times, whales remain elusive, continuously swimming and diving, surfacing only to breathe, and never allowing an opportunity for close inspection. Since we can't control the whales' behavior, we must take steps to control our own.

Whether close approaches by boats actually bother whales is open to debate. And since scientists are unable to distinguish disturbed behavior from normal behaviors, it is difficult to provide evidence of harassment. However, no one questions that vessels do strike and injure or kill whales. Researchers have compiled volumes of photographs showing the huge, spiraling gashes across the animals' bodies caused by collisions with boat propellers. Therefore, until our understanding of whales and our effect on them improves, we must keep our distance or risk loving them to death.

SEALS

Michael Payne, *National Marine Fisheries Service*

HARBOR SEALS AND GRAY SEALS are two of thirty-three species of pinnipeds ("fin-footed" animals), a suborder that includes seals, sea lions, and walruses. Both species occur in Sanctuary waters, yet the human visitor has little opportunity to make their acquaintance. Once a year-round resident, the harbor seal today occurs off the Massachusetts coast only seasonally, from mid-October through mid-May, prior to pupping season.

Harbor seals (*Phoca vitulina*) are among the most common marine mammals in the coastal waters of New England. Despite their abundance, seals' behavior and haunts in Massachusetts were known only by fishermen until recent decades. Throughout most of this century, harbor seals and their less locally abundant cousin, the gray seal (*Halichoerus grypus*), were considered pests.

Partly because of their curiosity around fishing boats, seals have always been perceived by fishermen as nuisances and competitors for their catch. From 1888 to 1962, Massachusetts offered a bounty on harbor seals to

An inquisitive harbor seal approaches a diver's flipper. If you're fortunate enough one day to come face to face with the wide-eyed stare of a harbor seal, you'll find the animal is likely to disappear with a punctuated splash, only to reappear within a few minutes, apparently too curious to resist the temptation to spy on the watcher. (Ed Lyman)

reduce their population, and increase the number of fish caught by fishermen. But by the early 1900s, when harbor seals had been nearly exterminated in certain areas, there was no noticeable effect on fish catches.

Harbor seals did not begin to make a comeback until after the bounty was lifted in 1962. Federal protection went into effect in 1972 under the Marine Mammal Protection Act, and since then, the number of harbor seals in southern New England has more than doubled. Seals appear to be long-lived animals, with a potential life span of thirty to forty years. Although now protected from hunting, harbor seals remain vulnerable to marine pollution, habitat destruction, or drowning in active or abandoned fishing nets.

Seal Pups

To bear their pups, adult seals often return to the same area where they were born. Most harbor seal pups are born from May to late June on isolated islands off the coasts of Maine and eastern Canada. The female bears her single pup on land. The pup can crawl and swim at birth. It enters the water almost immediately, and within three days it can dive. Nourished by its mother's high-calorie milk, the pup more than doubles its birth weight during the four to six weeks that it nurses.

Most seals abandon their pups following weaning, but harbor seal mothers may remain with their pups for longer periods. Once weaned, a pup will catch small schooling fish before proceeding to the adult diet of

More common in the Sanctuary during the winter and spring, the gray seal is distinguished from the harbor seal by its greater size (9 feet, or 2.7 meters), its highly arched Roman nose, and parallel nostrils. Seals are opportunistic feeders that search for easily caught prey—primarily the abundant sand lance and herring or other schooling fish. Adult gray seals consume 5 to 6 percent of their body weight, or about ten pounds (4.5 kg) daily. (Ed Lyman)

squid, invertebrates, and larger fishes. As with other seals, the female mates again shortly after the pups are weaned.

Each year, a few seals remain in Massachusetts waters throughout the summer, but thus far no rookeries—areas where seals congregate during the summer for breeding and pupping on an annual basis—have been established. The few pups seen in Cape Cod waters are probably stragglers from the rookeries to the northeast, or may be the result of premature births to inexperienced females. Very few of these pups survive.

To Haul Out or Not?

Seals have kept one foot, albeit a modified fin-foot, on land. The haul-out area is a land base where seals of all ages and both sexes can rest and find refuge during the non-breeding season.

Seals are practical creatures; they come ashore only if the conditions are right. The most densely populated haul-out locations near Cape Cod are on sandy shoals or sections of beach. At these locations, seals can drag themselves out of the water during any level of tide. However, most of the haul-out locations throughout New England are rocky ledges that are exposed only during low tide. Since their hind flippers are fixed in position and cannot be used for walking, seals have to drag themselves around on their bellies. They cannot climb the steep grades found on many rocky outcroppings. Instead, seals position themselves over submerged rocks as the tide ebbs, settling effortlessly onto a favorite rock as the water drops.

Generally the maximum number of seals at any location occurs within two hours of low tide on a sunny midday. Left undisturbed, the seals will remain on these rocks until the tide comes up again before they swim away. During high tide, seals feed and then return to their chosen haul-out to begin their daily cycle again.

In winter, hauling out on sandy shores or rocky ledges is a way to absorb some heat energy from the sun. The choice of whether or not to haul out is often temperature-dependent. For example, if the air temperature is warmer than that of the seawater, the seal will use less energy to keep warm by hauling out on a beach rather than staying in the water. However, if the wind is blowing more than 20 miles (32 km) per hour and the air temperature is below freezing, the seal will generally not haul out. Under these conditions, it is warmer to stay in the water.

In the late 1980s, approximately five thousand harbor seals lived along the Cape Cod coast during midwinter and early spring. Today, the largest haul-out location in the eastern United States is at Monomoy Island, south of Cape Cod. Approximately 1500 to 2000 seals can be seen there on afternoons when conditions are right.

Most haul-out sites are near sources of plentiful food. Common haul-out locations in midwinter or spring lie near several departure points for the Sanctuary, including the northern edge of Cape Cod at Race Point near Provincetown, the Duxbury Lighthouse and Guernet Point in Plymouth, the outer islands of Boston Harbor, and the small islands off Gloucester.

Currently, 75 percent of the winter seals in southern New England are located at Cape Cod and Nantucket sites. Knowing that a seal depends on its haul-out time to conserve energy, seal watchers should take special care not to disturb seals at their haul-outs. Close approaches will cause undue stress and send seals scattering.

Harbor seals haul out for rest, relaxation, and to sun themselves. They are the most common seal species sighted in the Sanctuary. (Richard Sears)

SEA TURTLES

Rarely seen in northern waters, the endangered hawksbill turtle (Eretmochelys imbricata) *continues to be hunted for its shell. Tortoiseshell is still carved into ornamental objects in many areas of the world.* (Ed Lyman)

S EA TURTLES ARE SHY CREATURES, so spotting one takes a discerning eye. At first glance, they appear to be ungainly relics from an ancient past, but this could not be further from the truth. Sea turtles are superbly adapted to life at sea. They are consummate swimmers, capable of flying unhindered through the water with powerful strokes of paddlelike fore flippers and by using the hind flippers as rudders. These same adaptations make them slow and vulnerable on land. Like all reptiles, they are air-breathing, and our occasional glimpse of them at the surface is fleeting—one or two minutes before they submerge for a prolonged dive.

Sea turtles are generally warm-water creatures, but some do travel to the cooler waters of the North Atlantic during some stage of their lives. Five species are found in Massachusetts waters: the leatherback, loggerhead, Kemp's ridley, Atlantic hawksbill, and green turtles. All have made appearances on Stellwagen Bank, but only three commonly use this region for foraging: the leatherback, loggerhead, and Kemp's ridley.

Sea turtles all have similar life histories. They spend their entire lives at sea, hauling out only to lay eggs on tropical beaches. Females of all five species lay clutches of about a hundred eggs and bury them in carefully concealed nests above the high tide line. After an incubation period of about two months, hatchlings dig their way to the surface of the sand and scramble over the beach into the surf.

Out of any single nest, perhaps only three individuals will survive to adulthood. Once in the ocean, they begin a perilous journey, spending their early lives near the surface in the offshore waters of the Atlantic or Gulf of Mexico. When fully grown, which may take several

A female sea turtle may deposit more than one hundred eggs in the sand along tropical beaches, but poachers, predators, and development take a heavy toll on hatching success. (Jack Woody)

decades, sea turtles return to their nesting beaches in the southeastern United States or Caribbean, repeating their epic journey every few years.

The Leatherback

The leatherback turtle (*Dermochelys coriacea*), cosmopolitan in its travels throughout the Atlantic, Pacific, and Indian oceans, is frequently encountered outside the tropics. It is known to range in the Atlantic as far north as Labrador, some 3100 miles (5000 km) from its tropical nesting beaches.

The leatherback, also variously called "trunkback" and "coffinback," is named for the black, rubbery skin covering its back, which takes the place of the usual hard shell of turtles. Individuals observed in our area are generally solitary adults, frequently measuring more than six

A leatherback hatchling scurries down to the surf. The interlude between hatching and swimming is its most vulnerable moment. (Jack Woody)

207

The largest of all living turtles, the leatherback can reach a length of seven feet (2.13 meters) and weigh over a ton (907.18 kg). Its back, or carapace, lacks the horny plates, or scutes, found on other sea turtles, and is distinguished by a series of seven raised ridges. (Sarah Landry)

feet (1.82 meters) in length and weighing over a thousand pounds (454.5 kg). They usually appear in the Gulf of Maine between May and June. In autumn, they travel farther offshore and begin their migration south for the winter.

The leatherback's distribution in northern waters coincides with jellyfish abundance. Like all sea turtles, the leatherback has no teeth, but its jaws are sharp-edged and its throat musculature highly developed to generate a powerful inflow of water as prey is sucked in. The esophagus, which may be nearly two meters long (6.56 feet), is lined with hundreds of flexible spines, all projecting toward the stomach, which help secure an otherwise slippery meal.

The leatherback is the deepest-diving marine reptile. Essentially pelagic, it is primarily a water-column feeder. As dusk approaches, the turtle executes shallower dives corresponding to the movement of comb jellies and other soft-bodied food species, which migrate to the upper surface layers at night. When dawn advances and daylight increases, the turtle's dives become increasingly deeper as its prey retreats from the light. Research suggests that during the day, the leatherback makes random

A HEAT-EXCHANGE SYSTEM

Sea turtles, like most other cold-blooded animals, lack an internal mechanism for regulating body temperatures. They depend on the temperature of their environment to keep their body temperature within an optimum range.

The leatherback, however, is unique among turtles. It has an elaborate heat-exchange system that allows the warm arterial blood leaving the body core to pass directly by the colder venous blood returning to the core. In this way, the incoming blood is warmed and blood leaving the body core is cooled. This mechanism keeps the core warmer than the periphery. Such a counter-current heat exchange adaptation allows the leatherback to maintain a deep body temperature of about 80°F (26.7°C), which lets it tolerate the polar waters near the Arctic Sea. Active leatherbacks have been reported in water temperatures believed to be below 43°F (6°C). No other reptile is known to remain active at this temperature.

dives in search of food or often basks at the surface, soaking up heat from the sun.

The Loggerhead

The loggerhead turtle (*Caretta caretta*), named for its disproportionately large head, conforms more to our idea of what a turtle should look like, because it has a heavy, bony shell. The reddish-brown carapace (upper shell) and yellowish plastron (lower shell) are covered by scutes —horny plates—arranged in a specific order, a convenient means of identifying the various turtle species.

Although loggerheads are the most numerous and widespread sea turtle species along the eastern seaboard, they make only marginal use of the Stellwagen Bank habitat. This threatened species cannot tolerate water temperatures much colder than those found around Stellwagen Bank. From midsummer through fall, limited sightings occur on Stellwagen Bank and Cape Cod Bay, as loggerheads disperse in search of the wide-ranging

COLD-STUNNING

In fall and winter, beach walkers may come upon a stranded ridley or loggerhead turtle. Although it may be immobile and appear dead, there is a strong likelihood that the turtle is alive but in shock, a victim of cold stunning. This is a condition similar to hypothermia in mammals.

Cold-stunning occurs if the turtle's body temperature drops below a critical level. As the temperature decreases, the turtle's movements become sluggish, its heartbeat slows, and its breathing rate drops. The turtle becomes unable to perform the normal swimming and feeding activities necessary to survive. Cold winds blow the turtles ashore and expose them to freezing temperatures.

A sea turtle found in this condition should not be put back into the water. Increasingly, rehabilitation at local nature centers is successful in saving the lives of these cold-stunning victims. With sea turtle populations at dangerously low levels, every individual saved is important. If you see a turtle on the beach, call New England Aquarium, in Boston, at (617) 973-5247.

bottom-dwelling invertebrates upon which they feed. Although difficult to see as adults, juvenile loggerheads are the most commonly found stranded turtle in Massachusetts.

The Kemp's Ridley

The Kemp's ridley, smallest of the sea turtles, has a broad, oval-shaped shell, usually a drab olive-gray. Occasionally a juvenile or sub-adult Kemp's ridley turtle (*Lepidochelys kempii*) is sighted on Stellwagen Bank. These juveniles are particularly susceptible to cold-stunning and frequently die from exposure. Studies suggest that the waters south of Cape Cod are generally the limit of their seasonal range. Recent tagging studies indicate that ridleys circle the Atlantic and then return to the Gulf of Mexico—where they were born—to lay their eggs. The scarcity of adult sightings in the Stellwagen Bank area

Sea turtles are in jeopardy worldwide. (Jack Woody)

suggests that the juveniles seen there are waifs lost to the population as they accidentally get trapped by the geographic barrier of Cape Cod.

Past, Present, and Future

Historically, all sea turtles have been valuable to humans. Within the past few decades, the high prices paid by consumer countries have put increased pressure on sea turtle populations. The leatherback, although widely reputed to be inedible, is slaughtered for meat, its oil rendered for caulking boats and for medicinal purposes, and its eggs eagerly sought for food. The skin of the ridley has been used recently for leather, and, like the loggerhead, the ridley serves as a source of meat, oil, and eggs for human consumption.

Sea turtle populations are in serious jeopardy. They are extremely susceptible to mortality from entanglement in fishing gear and ingestion of plastics and other human-generated debris. As important, the miles of beachfront property that are modified or developed each year result in a loss of nesting habitat. All species of sea turtles living in U.S. waters are listed as endangered or threatened under the Endangered Species Act of 1973.

Sea turtles have been traveling the seas unencumbered and virtually unchanged for more than 200 million years. The world they now inherit includes hazards for all stages of their nomadic life. A rare glimpse of one could be a last glimpse.

CONSERVATION ISSUES

Maureen Eldredge, Center for Marine Conservation

Proximity to the densely populated New England coast gives the Stellwagen Bank National Marine Sanctuary high visibility and allows many people to experience its magnificent natural wonders. However, its proximity also places it under a constant barrage of threats from human activities and pollution.

Bottlenose dolphins' exuberant leaps appear to be choreographed by some unseen maestro. These robust dolphins, which often approach boats and ride bow waves, are only rarely sighted in the Sanctuary. (Gina Reppucci)

The Challenge of a Multi-Use Sanctuary

The challenges of protecting a special habitat in a populated setting are many. Insults to the marine resources near urban areas can include dredge spoil dumping, sewage effluent outfalls, toxic and radioactive waste dis-

posal, marine debris, and tanker traffic, with the ever present threat of an oil spill. For years, Massachusetts Bay and other coastal habitats have been used as a dumping ground. Only recently has the general public become aware of the damage inflicted on our coastal environment by human activities.

National Marine Sanctuary status for Stellwagen Bank is only the first step in the process of increasing protection for its whales, fish, and their habitats. Sanctuary regulations prevent sand and gravel mining, prohibit ocean dumping within its boundaries, and give the National Oceanic and Atmospheric Administration some authority to regulate pollution sources outside the Sanctuary. But they do not stop all ocean pollution, nor can they erect a shield around the Sanctuary to protect it.

We have a long way to go before public awareness and concern for the ocean matches that for the land. It is too easy to dump our trash, toxins, and sewage at sea, out of sight. Changing marine policy depends on active public support and on awareness of the need to protect marine habitats.

The Stellwagen Bank National Marine Sanctuary is a sanctuary for all generations. Our success in protecting this spectacular area, and other special habitats along our coast, will continue to depend on the work of environmental organizations, legislators, and most important, the public.

Endangered Species

The dodo. The passenger pigeon. The snow leopard. The mountain gorilla. Sadly, these names are familiar to us because our presence on the planet either has erased theirs forever, or may do so in the near future.

Karen Steuer, U.S. House of Representatives Subcommittee on Environment and Natural Resources

Stories of extinction or near-extinction are global. Some of the species involved, such as the snow leopard, are distant and exotic. Others reside, or once resided, in our back yards. The passenger pigeon was once so numerous on the American plains that flocks passing overhead darkened the sky for days—but Martha, the last passenger pigeon, died in a Cincinnati zoo in 1914. Massachusetts settlers wrote in their journals that they

(Continued on page 216)

PLASTICS AFLOAT

Sharon Young

Every day, each American throws away over three pounds (1.36 kg) of trash. Every hour, over 2.5 million plastic beverage bottles are thrown away. Many of us are aware of the growing crisis in landfills, but many don't know about the growing crisis of ocean garbage. The Stellwagen Bank National Marine Sanctuary is bounded by heavily settled areas of Massachusetts. Waste generated by river runoff, beach pollution, sewage and waste disposal, as well as carelessly handled boat refuse, is creating a hazard for the residents of the Sanctuary.

Scientists believe that plastic trash is the most widespread threat facing many marine species. Think twice before carelessly throwing away trash; the consequences are bad, both for economies dependent on the sea and for wildlife. Commercial fishermen log downtime because of encounters with marine garbage. Even apparently benign objects, such as styrofoam pieces or cigarette filters, can become death traps for ocean dwellers that mistake them for food.

The quality of the marine environment depends directly on human actions. Shore residents and visitors can also help the problem of ocean garbage by reducing the volume of refuse. Those of us who do not live close to the shore can help the problem of degradation of ocean habitats by advocating reduced use of chemical pesticides, which often find their way into river runoff and eventually degrade ocean habitats.

What's Wrong With This Picture?

• *Lost nets and abandoned traps "ghost fish," continuing to catch finfish and shellfish that are never retrieved by fishermen.*

• *Entanglements in large nets can cause drowning; snagging smaller pieces of net can restrict body movement, leading to exhaustion and starvation.*

• *A simple opening in a plastic six-pack holder becomes a noose around the neck of a sea bird.*

• *Sea turtles mistake balloons and plastic bags for jellyfish. The indigestible material blocks the normal passage of food, causing the turtle's slow and agonizing death.*

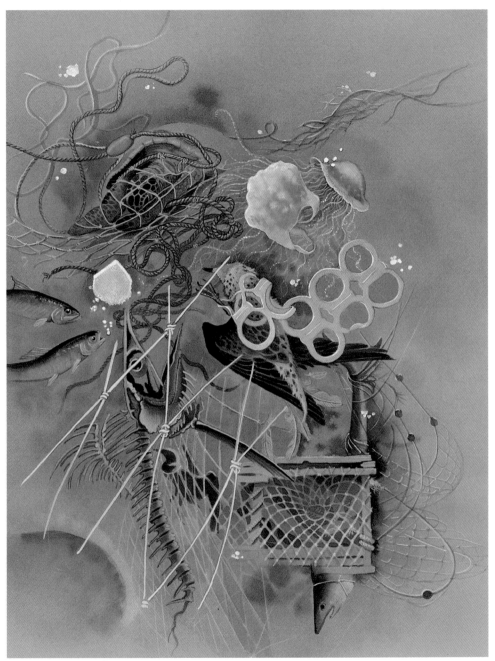

(Sarah Landry)

In the early 1800s the roseate tern had numerous nesting colonies as far north as Nova Scotia. Hunted for their feathers, which were cherished in the millinery trade, the birds were severely depleted by the 1880s and remain endangered today.
(D.C. Twichell, Manomet Bird Observatory)

felt they could almost walk across Cape Cod Bay on the backs of right whales—but today the North Atlantic right whale teeters on the brink of extinction.

It is for species like these that Congress passed the Endangered Species Act in 1973. It was, and still is, a landmark conservation law, the keystone of wildlife protection in the United States and a model for the rest of the world. Protecting thousands, perhaps millions, of plant and animal species from the looming threat of extinction may be one of the most difficult challenges humans face today. Increasing human population and rapid technological advancements, frequently developed without thought for their long-term ecological consequences, accelerate the extinction process.

All species are adapted to their own niches in an ecosystem, whether the habitat is a tropical rain forest, the top of the Himalayas, or the edge of Stellwagen Bank. In effect, plant and animal species are the building blocks of ecosystems. Like stacks of building blocks, we can remove a few from the stack, or replace them with blocks of similar size and shape, and the stack will remain intact. For example, if a leatherback turtle's favorite meal of jellyfish is in short supply, it can satisfy its appetite with squid or other soft-shelled mollusks. If a humpback whale can't find herring, then mackerel or sand lance will do just as well.

The Stellwagen Bank ecosystem, like any other, has its own building blocks, some of which are listed under the Endangered Species Act as either endangered (in danger of extinction) or threatened (likely to become endangered within the foreseeable future). Most obvious among them are the great whales: the North Atlantic right whale, humpback whale, finback whale, sei whale, and blue whale.

The endangered status of the whales was originally a result of decades or centuries of commercial whaling, but these fascinating animals face very different threats today. While some whales, like the humpback, appear to be increasing in numbers, thanks to their protected status, the North Atlantic right whale population is not, even though it has been protected from hunting since

1935. What key factors are we missing in our efforts to help this species survive? Have we pulled some essential building block out of the ecosystem, an element crucial to this animal's ability to thrive?

Right whales are more specialized feeders than most other whales. Is it possible that we have upset a delicate marine food web balance and forced the right whale to compete with other species for its food? Most important, will we be able to identify the problem in time to prevent the right whale from going the way of the passenger pigeon? Or will future visitors to Stellwagen Bank be denied even the most remote possibility of seeing a right whale in Massachusetts waters?

Sea turtles join the whales on the list. The leatherback, Kemp's ridley, and hawksbill sea turtles are considered endangered, while the loggerhead and the green turtle are listed as threatened.

The leatherback turtle is truly a miracle of evolution—a species so perfectly designed for its environment that improving it would be unthinkable. Unfortunately, while two hundred million years of evolution have left

A finback mother and calf, named Hope and Future, symbolize an optimistic outlook. The calf will remain with its mother for almost a year. About twenty feet at birth, it nurses on milk rich in fat and protein, doubling its birth length within six months. (Bill Rossiter)

217

leatherback turtles so perfectly designed for their niche in the marine ecosystem, it has not designed them to deal with humans. Human harvest of turtle eggs and development of their tropical nesting beaches still threaten turtles in many parts of the world. Those of us lucky enough to glimpse a seven-foot (5-meter) adult leatherback turtle at sea will find it difficult to believe that they begin as three-inch (7.5-cm) hatchlings on tropical beaches—the same beautiful white beaches that attract vacation resorts. Federal laws protect these turtles when they come to feed on Stellwagen Bank, but international cooperation is needed to save their nesting habitats.

The protection afforded all these species under the Endangered Species Act is enhanced by the designation of the Stellwagen Bank National Marine Sanctuary. Like the Endangered Species Act, national marine sanctuaries are designed to let humans and wildlife coexist. Their goals are essentially the same: to enrich our lives and the lives of those who inherit the planet after us.

Critical Habitat for Migrating Species

Peter L. Tyack, Woods Hole Oceanographic Institution

What does it mean to put borders around a small marine sanctuary? Organisms that settle on the ocean bottom are tied to a particular piece of real estate just as many terrestrial organisms are. However, most other marine life moves with the water, which flows in and out of any sanctuary border.

Many of the whales, large fish, and sea birds which use Stellwagen Bank are highly mobile, migrating thousands of kilometers annually and moving hundreds of kilometers within days. They sample huge areas of ocean to select particular features of the habitat for feeding or other activities. For example, North Atlantic right whales search for high concentrations of prey species so they can feed most efficiently. Because of variation either in the physical environment or in the dynamics of prey populations, an area like Stellwagen Bank differs in value as a feeding habitat from year to year. In good years, 200 to 350 humpback whales may feed there, while in other years, there may be only a few resident humpbacks.

We are just beginning to understand what environmental features make whale habitats particularly good or bad. Research is urgently needed to define critical attributes of habitat for each endangered species. These attributes include positive features such as availability of prey as well as negative features such as chemical or noise pollution.

Habitat requirements for whales are like the complex system required for modern aviation. Jets are free to cover most of the globe. While they seem free from earth, they require specialized communication and navigation gear on the ground, as well as ground services such as landing strips and fuel supplies. No one landing field is critical; if Logan is closed, a jet can redirect to Providence or Hartford. However, a generous number of alternatives are required to prevent potential disasters. Similarly, a whale migrating north in the spring from its winter breeding grounds may not happen to choose Stellwagen Bank as a prime feeding habitat this year, but may instead divert to other areas. Whales probably need several areas like Stellwagen Bank to choose among in order to feed well each year. This is the sense in which Stellwagen Bank is a critical habitat to migratory oppor-

Belly to belly, two North Atlantic right whales spyhop, lifting their heads out of the water. Habitat protection is critical for migratory species such as the North Atlantic right whale as well as sea turtles, sea birds, and many other marine species. (Bob Bowman)

tunistic feeders. While its protection is an important first step, we must recognize that the whales we see in Stellwagen may cover much of the western North Atlantic. Conservation of these migratory species requires protection of a web of different habitats and environmental features.

Russell DeConti, Center for Coastal Studies

An Ocean Flows Through It

One of the main objectives of a marine sanctuary is to provide a safe haven for the myriad of sea creatures that find shelter, food, and breeding habitat within its waters and bottom environments. However, ocean sanctuaries suffer one disadvantage over their terrestrial counterparts: no obvious features distinguish them from their surroundings.

On Stellwagen Bank, there are no obvious borders or points of entry and no physical barriers to protect the inhabitants from the "outside" world. In fact, the inhabitants of the Sanctuary are continually changing, moving in and out in response to the tides, seasons, and annual migrations. The sanctuary is never the same, with its boundaries fixed mainly in our minds and an ocean, quite literally, flowing through them.

Protecting an environment of such dynamic and transient qualities presents special challenges. First, there is the need to create an identity, or sense of place, for the Sanctuary in order to increase public awareness of its special values and its importance as a marine habitat. Since much of what happens occurs beneath the surface of the water, our vision of the Sanctuary is quite limited. Beyond the vague notion that this is a special place, a notion largely due to the presence of whales, the Sanctuary may at times appear faceless and difficult to distinguish from the rest of the ocean.

However, the careful observer will learn that Stellwagen has many faces, each one an aspect of the complex interactions between the physical, chemical, and biological factors that create the cycles of oceanic life. From the tiniest plankton, whose populations explode in the spring when bathed in sunlight and nutrient-rich waters, to the schools of sand lance, which swarm into the dense clouds of zooplankton to feed and ultimately be fed upon by the baleen whales and basking sharks, the natural order of things reveals itself in subtle displays of life and death, death and life. Thus, the Sanctuary's identity is linked to these natural cycles that have evolved over thousands of years, as well as to the relatively short-term changes in the seasons, seawater chemistry, and abundance of predator and prey species.

This tentative balance may be upset, or even destroyed, by our careless disregard for the ocean and its inhabitants. Chemical contaminants enter the bay from many sources, including runoff from the land, river discharges (some from as far away as Maine), and precipitation. In addition, direct ocean disposal of materials such as dredged spoils and sewage effluent and accidental spills from the transport of chemical and petroleum products also threaten the Sanctuary Minute amounts of toxic substances such as lead, copper, mercury, DDT, PCBs, and many of the synthetic organic compounds (mainly solvents and pesticides) can accumulate in the tissues of some marine organisms, leading to tumors, physical and genetic abnormalities, and concerns about seafood safety. Although disposal of such materials is prohibited within the Sanctuary, contaminants may be carried by ocean currents to natural depositional areas, such as Stellwagen Basin, where long-term accumulations may affect water quality, sediments, and marine organisms. All these factors must be carefully monitored and regulated in order to protect Sanctuary resources.

The challenges we must face at the Sanctuary level are, in fact, no more or less daunting than those that we must face globally if we are to live in harmony with the ocean. Our view of our relationship to this environment will need to change greatly as we adjust our activities to the tolerances of the sea. The Sanctuary represents a unique opportunity to find that elusive balance between humans and nature. If workable concepts for conservation and stewardship can be developed and embraced within the Stellwagen Bank Sanctuary, there is hope for the rest of the ocean.

The ocean follows no boundaries, nor do its many inhabitants. Stellwagen Bank National Marine Sanctuary is a sanctuary for all generations. (Alan Hudson)

INDEX